RYA Astro Navigation Handbook

by Melanie Bartlett F.R.I.N.

2009

© Melanie Bartlett
First Published 2009
Reprinted 2011, September 2013
September 2014, May 2015, September 2016,
September 2017, September 2018, January 2020,
January 2021, January 2022, July 2023, November 2024
The Royal Yachting Association
RYA House, Ensign Way, Hamble,
Southampton SO31 4YA
Tel: 02380 604 100
Web: www.rya.org.uk

We welcome feedback on our publications at
publications@rya.org.uk

You can check content updates for
RYA publications at
www.rya.org.uk/go/bookschangelog

ISBN: 978-1-906435-09-7
RYA Order Code: G78

All rights reserved. No part of this publication may be reproduced, stored in a retrieval system, or transmitted, in any form or by any means, electronic, mechanical, photocopying, recording or otherwise, without the prior permission in writing of the publishers.

A CIP record of this book is available from the British Library. Telephone 02380 604 100 for a free copy of our Publications Catalogue.

Note: While all reasonable care has been taken in the preparation of this book, the publisher takes no responsibility for the use of the methods or products or contracts described in the book.

Acknowledgements: Mike Linsky and John Rogers
Cover Design: Pete Galvin
Illustrations: Melanie Bartlett
Typeset: Creativebyte
Proofreading, index and glossary: Alan Thatcher
Printed in the UK

Contents

1	Five-Minute Astro	5
2	All Done By Mirrors - The Sextant	7
3	The Celestial Sphere	14
4	Time	19
5	The Noon Sight	28
6	Morning and Afternoon Sun Sights	33
7	Planets	43
8	Morning and Evening Stars	52
9	Polaris	61
10	The Moon	64
	Appendix 1 - Plotting Sheets	69
	Glossary	71
	Index	72
	Notes	75

Introduction

It's hard to argue that astro navigation is essential. You could buy a perfectly good GPS set for the money you might spend on astro reference books alone, and several back-ups for the price of a decent sextant.

But there is something enormously satisfying about handling a sextant, and using a piece of Georgian technology for its intended purpose. And there's a kind of freemasonry about astro: a sense that until you've been initiated into its secrets and mysteries, you're not quite a proper Navigator.

The funny thing is that although a lot of astro jargon has an almost mystical ring about it, most of us already know the "secrets" on which the whole science of astro navigation is based.

Chapter 1: Five-Minute Astro

The basics

Imagine, for a moment, that you are somewhere in open water, with a single bright star directly overhead.

Astronomers have spent centuries watching, recording, and predicting the movement of stars, and the results of their efforts are published in star charts and almanacs. So if you can identify which star you are looking at, you can find out where it is.

And if you know where the star is, you know where you are.

But suppose the star isn't directly overhead?

If it's almost directly above you, then you must be somewhere fairly close to the spot at which it is directly overhead. And if it's low on the horizon, then you must be a long way away.

If we could measure, accurately, the angle between the star and our **zenith** (a point in the sky that is immediately overhead), we could be more precise than "fairly close" or "a long way away" because – as a rule of thumb – every degree corresponds to sixty miles.

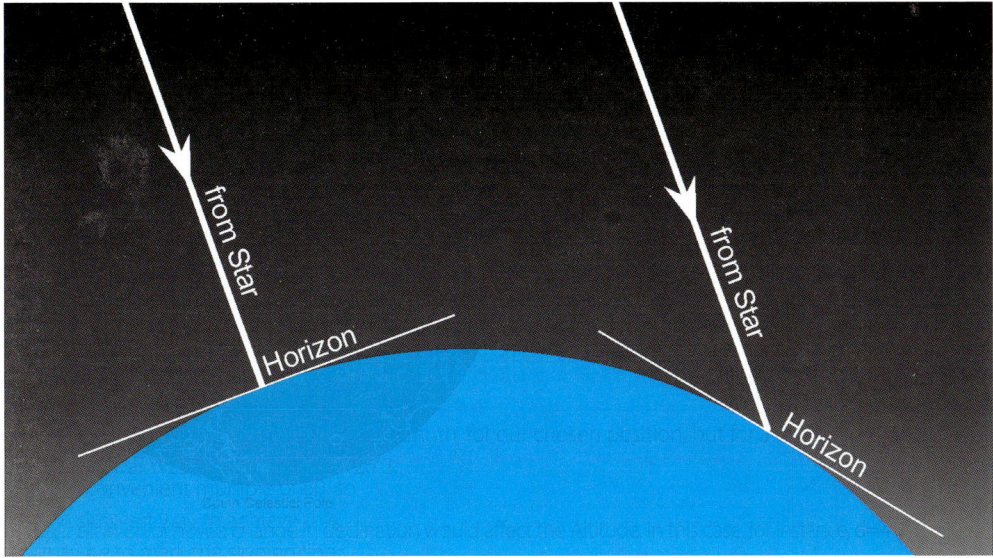

As you move away from the point at which a star is directly overhead, the star appears to sink towards the horizon.

Astro Navigation Handbook | 5

Unfortunately, it's very difficult to be absolutely certain where the zenith is. But it's relatively easy to measure the angle between a star and the horizon, to a high level of accuracy.

Suppose, for instance, that there's a star directly over London, and another directly over New York, and that to us they appear to be 70° above our north-east horizon and 50° above the horizon in the north-west (see illustration).

Being seventy degrees above the horizon means that the London star is twenty degrees away from directly overhead. Using the "one degree is sixty miles" rule, this means that we must be somewhere on the perimeter of a circle whose centre is directly below the star, and whose radius is 1200 miles.

Applying the same logic to the New York star means that we are also on another circle whose radius of 2400 miles and whose centre is in New York.

There are only two places where we can possibly be on both circles at once – and as one of them is off Iceland and the other is off the Azores, it shouldn't be too difficult to tell which is which!

So the principle of astro navigation is quite straightforward:
Measuring the altitude of a body above the horizon tells us how far we are from the point at which that body is directly overhead.

To put it into practice, there are just three problems to overcome:-
- measuring the angle between the heavenly body and the horizon to an accuracy of a fraction of a degree.
- knowing where the heavenly body was at the moment the angle was measured.
- drawing circles with radiuses of hundreds of miles.

Chapter 2: All Done By Mirrors - The Sextant

The most fundamental measurement in astro navigation is the angle between the horizon and a heavenly body such as the sun, or a star – known as its **altitude**. Mariners have used all sorts of contraptions for the purpose, but for the past two and a half centuries, the first choice has been a sextant.

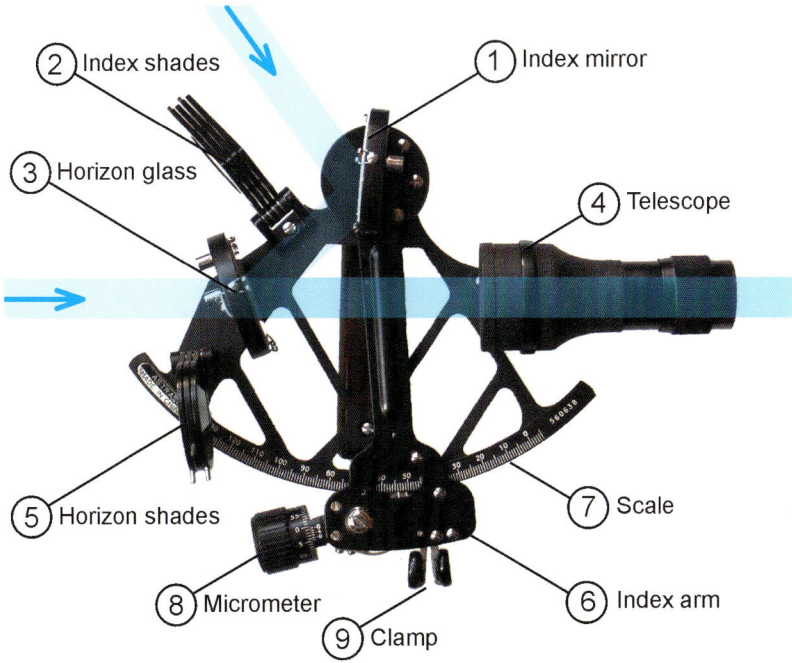

How a sextant works

Light from the sun, star, or planet is reflected from the index mirror (1), through various removable shades (2), to the horizon glass (3), which reflects it into the telescope (4).

On a "split view" sextant, the horizon glass is half mirror and half plain glass, so the user, looking through the telescope, can see the reflected image of the heavenly body in the silvered half, but can also see the horizon through the plain glass. Another set of shades – the horizon shades (5) – is provided to reduce glare from the surface of the water.

On an "all-view" sextant, the horizon glass isn't split. Instead, it has an all-over coating that reflects like a mirror, but lets you see through it at the same time.

Whichever type of horizon glass you have, the end result is that you can look in two directions at once, adjusting the angle between the two lines of sight by moving the index arm (6), and reading off the angle on the scale (7) and the micrometer drum (8).

Every complete turn of the micrometer drum moves the line of sight by just one degree, so it's very good at making small, precisely controlled movements. But it would be tedious – to put it mildly – if it took fifty turns of the micrometer to change the angle by fifty degrees. To save time and temper, the micrometer can be disengaged by squeezing the clamp (9). The index arm then pivots freely until the micrometer is re-engaged by releasing the clamp.

Shooting the sun

To "shoot" the sun, hold the handle of the sextant in your right hand, set the index arm to approximately zero, and adjust the telescope to suit your eyesight by focusing it on some distant object such as the horizon.

Swing most of the index and horizon shades into place, and then look through the telescope, straight at the sun. You should see two images, probably not quite lined up with each other.

Now comes the tricky bit: squeeze the clamp on the index arm, and push it away from you, simultaneously tilting the body of the sextant downwards until the telescope is looking straight at the horizon. You will almost certainly have to move some of the horizon shades out of the way, but the idea is to keep the reflected image of the sun in view until it is superimposed on the direct image of the horizon.

Then let go of the clamp, and turn the micrometer drum to tweak the two images until the sun appears to just touch the horizon. Check that the sextant is vertical by rocking it gently from side to side: the reflected sun should just brush the horizon in the middle of each swing, without dipping below it.

ALL DONE BY MIRRORS - THE SEXTANT

CHAPTER 2

Shooting stars or planets

The principle of shooting stars or planets (or the moon) is, of course exactly the same, except that you don't need the shades. The main difference is that small and relatively dim objects are much more difficult to keep in view as you bring the reflected image down to the horizon. One solution is to use the sextant "upside down".

1. Set it to zero, and adjust it to suit your eyesight as usual, but hold it in your left hand, with the index mirror at the bottom and the micrometer and clamp at the top.

2. Find the star or planet in the telescope, then squeeze the clamp and push the index arm away from you. This time, though, do not tilt the sextant downwards but keep the telescope pointing straight at the star or planet. The idea is that you are going to bring the horizon up to the star, instead of bringing the star down to the horizon.

3. As soon as you've got the star and horizon in view simultaneously, you can turn the sextant up the right way, and carry on as usual.

Reading the Sextant

Reading a sextant is a three-stage process, involving the main scale, the micrometer drum, and the Vernier scale.

- The main scale gives the number of whole degrees
- The micrometer shows the number of minutes (sixtieths of a degree) and
- The Vernier indicates the number of tenths of a minute

In the photograph, for instance, the reading on the main scale is just past 57.

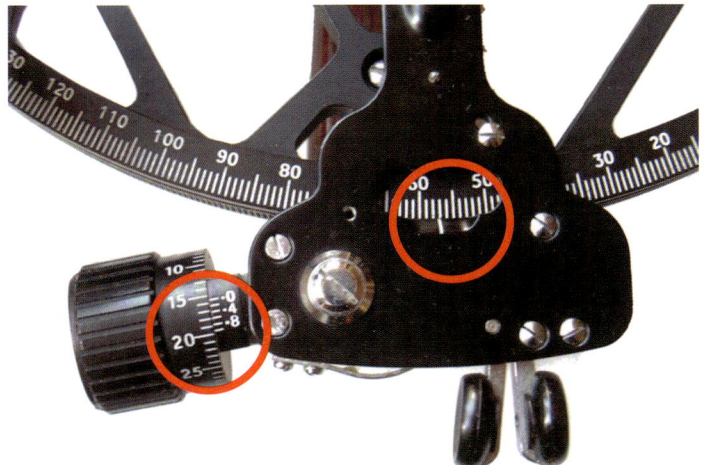

Take the reading on the micrometer drum that is alongside the "zero" mark of the Vernier scale. In this case, the reading is between 15 and 16, so the micrometer reading is 15'.

For tenths of a minute, look for the mark on the Vernier scale that is closest to being lined up with a mark on the micrometer drum. In the photo, it's the 0.6 mark, so the sextant reading is 57°15'.6.

Astro Navigation Handbook

Adjusting a Sextant

It only takes a few minutes to check and adjust a sextant, but the results are well worth it.

Perpendicularity

Perpendicularity checks that the index mirror is perpendicular to the frame.

- Remove the telescope, and squeeze the clamp in order to set the index arm to about twenty degrees.
- Then hold the instrument with its frame roughly horizontal and the index mirror nearest to your eye, so that you are looking past the index mirror, towards the "zero" end of the scale beyond it. At the same time, you'll see the other end of the scale reflected in the mirror.
- The two parts of the scale should line up with each other to form a smooth, even curve. If they don't, tweak the adjusting screw on the index mirror until they do.

ALL DONE BY MIRRORS - THE SEXTANT

CHAPTER 2

Side error

Side error arises when the horizon glass is not perpendicular to the frame. The effect is to offset the reflected image sideways from the direct image.

By day, the simplest way to check and correct side error is to fit the telescope back onto the sextant, and look through it towards the horizon. Adjust the index arm by twiddling the micrometer screw until the direct and reflected images of the horizon are perfectly lined up with each other. Then tip the sextant on its side: the two images of the horizon should stay lined up with each other. If you see two horizons, move them back into line with each other by adjusting one of the two screws on the horizon glass. Usually (but not always), the one that handles side error is the one furthest from the main frame of the sextant.

At night, a better way is to fit the telescope and look through it towards a bright star. Adjust the index arm by twiddling the micrometer screw until the direct and reflected images of the star are side by side, then adjust the screw on the horizon glass until they are perfectly superimposed on each other.

Astro Navigation Handbook | 11

Index error

The third and most important sextant check is for index error. It happens if the mirrors aren't parallel to each other when the instrument reads zero. It's worth getting into the habit of checking it every time you use the sextant.

Set the index arm so that it is reading precisely zero, with the mark on the index arm against the zero mark on the scale, and the micrometer also reading zero. Then, holding it in the usual operating position – look at the horizon. If you see two horizons, try to make them coincide by tweaking the remaining screw on the horizon glass.

At night, you can achieve the same thing (and with even greater precision) by lining up the two images of a star instead of the horizon.

There's no need to remove index error altogether. When you've got it nearly right, tweak the micrometer screw until the two horizons coincide, and note the reading. This residual "index error" can always be applied as a correction to the eventual sight.

ALL DONE BY MIRRORS - THE SEXTANT

CHAPTER 2

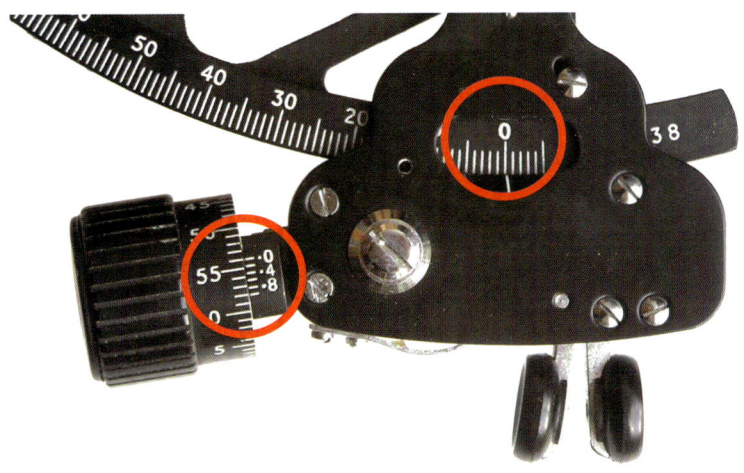

Notice that in the photo, the main scale appears to be reading 0, but the micrometer says 54'. To set the sextant to read precisely 00', we would have to increase the reading by 6'. In other words, this sextant is under-reading by 6', so we have to add 6' to every measurement.

Index error is often described as being "on the arc" or "off the arc". If the error is "on the arc", it means that the index arm is "on the arc" (i.e. showing a positive reading) when it should be zero. In the photograph, where it is showing a negative reading, it is "off the arc". The words "on" and "off" make it easy to remember how to perform the correction:
- If the error is off, add it back on
- If the error is on, take it off

Tricks of the trade
- *In clear weather, make the horizon even crisper by taking sights from as high on the boat as possible*
- *In mist or haze, make the horizon closer and clearer by taking sights from as low in the boat as possible*
- *Except for a noon sight, take several sights of the same body in quick succession, and take an average of the results*
- *Generally, take star or planet sights as soon after sunset or as late before sunrise as possible, when the horizon is clearest*

Within a couple of days of full moon, it may be possible to take star or planet sights by moonlight – but only when the moon is high in the sky.

Chapter 3: The Celestial Sphere

Five hundred years ago, Copernicus suggested that the Earth was not the centre of the Universe. Four hundred years ago Galileo proved it.

But for navigators, it's extremely inconvenient. As a matter of simple pragmatism, we still base our calculations on the assumption that the sun, stars, and planets are all on the inner surface of a vast celestial sphere.

The celestial sphere spins around the **North and South celestial poles**, which are perfectly lined up with the Earth's North and South poles, and it has a **celestial equator** midway between them. It, too, is perfectly lined up with its counterpart on Earth.

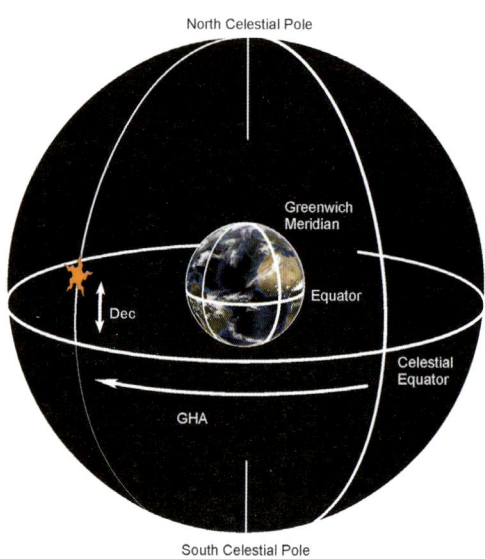

The celestial equivalent of latitude is called **Declination** (Dec). Like latitude, it is measured in degrees, north or south of the Equator, but as a matter of convention, it is usually written with the hemisphere (North or South) before the numbers, rather than after them.

The celestial equivalent of longitude is called **Greenwich Hour Angle (GHA)** but instead of being measured east or west of the prime meridian, it's always measured westwards.

So when the Sun is directly overhead at Barbados, whose latitude and longitude are 13°N 59°W, its GHA must be 59° and its declination N13°.

If its GHA were 192° and its Dec were S18°, it would be overhead at Vanuatu (18°S 168°E).

Zenith

*It's not just the north and south poles and the equator that have counterparts on both the celestial and terrestrial spheres. Every point on the Earth's surface has a corresponding point on the celestial sphere, called its **zenith**.*

To an observer on the surface of the Earth, their zenith is the point that appears to be directly overhead, whose Declination and GHA correspond with their own latitude and longitude.

THE CELESTIAL SPHERE

CHAPTER 3

Finding the Greenwich Hour Angle of the Sun

Data for the Sun, Moon, and visible planets are published in books such as **The Nautical Almanac**, or in civilian publications such as Reeds Astro Navigation Tables.

Suppose, for instance, that we need to know the Sun's GHA at 09:34:12 UT 21 September:-

The so-called **Daily Page** (really the Daily spread!) of the Nautical Almanac actually includes data for three days, and for several different bodies, but the information for the Sun on the 21st is easy to find, on the left hand side of the right hand page, where it shows the GHA and Declination for every hour.

UT	SUN G.H.A.	Dec.	MOON G.H.A.	v	Dec.	d	H.P.	Lat.	Twilight Naut.	Civil	Sunrise	Moonrise 21	22	23	24
	° ′	° ′	° ′	′	° ′	′	′	°	h m	h m	h m	h m	h m	h m	h m
								N 72	02 59	04 30	05 39	19 07	18 51	18 39	18 28
21 00	181 42.7 N 0 43.9		47 45.2	7.4	S16 53.3	6.4	59.0	N 70	03 19	04 38	05 40	18 36	18 33	18 30	18 27
01	196 42.9	42.9	62 11.6	7.4	16 46.9	6.5	59.0	68	03 34	04 45	05 41	18 14	18 19	18 23	18 25
02	211 43.1	42.0	76 38.0	7.3	16 40.4	6.7	59.0	66	03 47	04 51	05 42	17 56	18 08	18 16	18 24
03	226 43.4 ··	41.0	91 04.3	7.4	16 33.7	6.7	59.1	64	03 57	04 55	05 43	17 41	17 58	18 11	18 23
04	241 43.6	40.0	105 30.7	7.3	16 27.0	6.8	59.1	62	04 05	04 59	05 44	17 29	17 50	18 07	18 22
05	256 43.8	39.1	119 57.0	7.4	16 20.2	7.0	59.2	60	04 12	05 03	05 44	17 18	17 42	18 03	18 21
06	271 44.0 N 0 38.1		134 23.4	7.3	S16 13.2	7.1	59.2	N 58	04 18	05 06	05 45	17 09	17 36	17 59	18 20
07	286 44.2	37.1	148 49.7	7.3	16 06.1	7.2	59.2	56	04 24	05 08	05 45	17 01	17 30	17 56	18 20
08	301 44.5	36.1	163 16.0	7.4	15 58.9	7.3	59.3	54	04 28	05 10	05 46	16 54	17 25	17 53	18 19
09	316 44.7 ··	35.2	177 42.4	7.3	15 51.6	7.4	59.3	52	04 32	05 12	05 46	16 47	17 21	17 51	18 19
U 10	331 44.9	34.2	192 08.7	7.3	15 44.2	7.5	59.4	50	04 36	05 14	05 46	16 41	17 16	17 48	18 18
N 11	346 45.1	33.2	206 35.0	7.3	15 36.7	7.6	59.4	45	04 43	05 18	05 47	16 29	17 07	17 43	18 17
D 12	1 45.3 N 0 32.2		221 01.3	7.3	S15 29.1	7.7	59.4	N 40	04 49	05 20	05 48	16 18	17 00	17 39	18 16
A 13	16 45.6	31.3	235 27.6	7.3	15 21.4	7.9	59.5	35	04 53	05 23	05 48	16 09	16 53	17 35	18 15
Y 14	31 45.8	30.3	249 53.9	7.3	15 13.5	7.9	59.5	30	04 57	05 24	05 48	16 01	16 47	17 32	18 15
15	46 46.0 ··	29.3	264 20.2	7.3	15 05.6	8.1	59.5	20	05 01	05 27	05 49	15 47	16 37	17 26	18 14
16	61 46.2	28.4	278 46.5	7.3	14 57.5	8.1	59.6	N 10	05 04	05 28	05 49	15 35	16 29	17 21	18 13
17	76 46.5	27.4	293 12.8	7.3	14 49.4	8.3	59.6	0	05 05	05 29	05 49	15 24	16 20	17 16	18 12
18	91 46.7 N 0 26.4		307 39.1	7.3	S14 41.1	8.4	59.7	S 10	05 04	05 29	05 50	15 13	16 12	17 11	18 11
19	106 46.9	25.4	322 05.4	7.2	14 32.7	8.4	59.7	20	05 02	05 28	05 50	15 01	16 03	17 06	18 10
20	121 47.1	24.5	336 31.6	7.3	14 24.3	8.6	59.7	30	04 58	05 26	05 49	14 47	15 53	17 00	18 09
21	136 47.3 ··	23.5	350 57.9	7.3	14 15.7	8.7	59.8	35	04 55	05 24	05 49	14 39	15 47	16 57	18 08
22	151 47.6	22.5	5 24.2	7.3	14 07.0	8.8	59.8	40	04 51	05 22	05 49	14 30	15 40	16 53	18 07
23	166 47.8	21.5	19 50.5	7.3	13 58.2	8.9	59.8	45	04 45	05 20	05 49	14 19	15 33	16 49	18 07
22 00	181 48.0 N 0 20.6		34 16.8	7.3	S13 49.3	8.9	59.9	S 50	04 39	05 17	05 49	14 06	15 23	16 44	18 06
01	196 48.2	19.6	48 43.1	7.3	13 40.4	9.1	59.9	52	04 35	05 15	05 49	14 00	15 19	16 41	18 05
02	211 48.4	18.6	63 09.4	7.3	13 31.3	9.2	59.9	54	04 31	05 13	05 48	13 53	15 14	16 39	18 05
03	226 48.7 ··	17.7	77 35.7	7.3	13 22.1	9.3	60.0	56	04 27	05 11	05 48	13 46	15 09	16 36	18 04
04	241 48.9	16.7	92 02.0	7.3	13 12.8	9.3	60.0	58	04 22	05 09	05 48	13 37	15 03	16 32	18 04

From this, we can see that at 09:00, the GHA was 316°44′.7, and that it is increasing at about fifteen degrees per hour. This is because the Sun is "going round the Earth" once every 24 hours, and 360 degrees in 24 hours works out at fifteen degrees per hour.

Knowing how quickly the GHA is changing means that it is just a matter of arithmetic to work out how much it has changed between 09:00 (the time given in the tables) and 09:34:12 (the time we are interested in).

Astro Navigation Handbook | 15

It's not the kind of sum that most of us could do in our heads, though, so to make life easier and more accurate, the Nautical Almanac and its commercial rivals include tables of **Increments and Corrections.**

INCREMENTS AND CORRECTIONS

34ᵐ SUN PLANETS	ARIES	MOON	v or Corrⁿ d	v or Corrⁿ d	v or Corrⁿ d	35ᵐ SUN PLANETS	ARIES	MOON	v or Corrⁿ d	v or Corrⁿ d	v or Corrⁿ d
s ° ′	° ′	° ′	′ ′	′ ′	′ ′	s ° ′	° ′	° ′	′ ′	′ ′	′ ′
00 8 30·0	8 31·4	8 06·8	0·0 0·0	6·0 3·5	12·0 6·9	00 8 45·0	8 46·4	8 21·1	0·0 0·0	6·0 3·6	12·0 7·1
01 8 30·3	8 31·6	8 07·0	0·1 0·1	6·1 3·5	12·1 7·0	01 8 45·3	8 46·7	8 21·3	0·1 0·1	6·1 3·6	12·1 7·2
02 8 30·5	8 31·9	8 07·2	0·2 0·1	6·2 3·6	12·2 7·0	02 8 45·5	8 46·9	8 21·6	0·2 0·1	6·2 3·7	12·2 7·2
03 8 30·8	8 32·1	8 07·5	0·3 0·2	6·3 3·6	12·3 7·1	03 8 45·8	8 47·2	8 21·8	0·3 0·2	6·3 3·7	12·3 7·3
04 8 31·0	8 32·4	8 07·7	0·4 0·2	6·4 3·7	12·4 7·1	04 8 46·0	8 47·4	8 22·0	0·4 0·2	6·4 3·8	12·4 7·3
05 8 31·3	8 32·6	8 08·0	0·5 0·3	6·5 3·7	12·5 7·2	05 8 46·3	8 47·7	8 22·3	0·5 0·3	6·5 3·8	12·5 7·4
06 8 31·5	8 32·9	8 08·2	0·6 0·3	6·6 3·8	12·6 7·2	06 8 46·5	8 47·9	8 22·5	0·6 0·4	6·6 3·9	12·6 7·5
07 8 31·8	8 33·2	8 08·4	0·7 0·4	6·7 3·9	12·7 7·3	07 8 46·8	8 48·2	8 22·8	0·7 0·4	6·7 4·0	12·7 7·5
08 8 32·0	8 33·4	8 08·7	0·8 0·5	6·8 3·9	12·8 7·4	08 8 47·0	8 48·4	8 23·0	0·8 0·5	6·8 4·0	12·8 7·6
09 8 32·3	8 33·7	8 08·9	0·9 0·5	6·9 4·0	12·9 7·4	09 8 47·3	8 48·7	8 23·2	0·9 0·5	6·9 4·1	12·9 7·6
10 8 32·5	8 33·9	8 09·2	1·0 0·6	7·0 4·0	13·0 7·5	10 8 47·5	8 48·9	8 23·5	1·0 0·6	7·0 4·1	13·0 7·7
11 8 32·8	8 34·2	8 09·4	1·1 0·6	7·1 4·1	13·1 7·5	11 8 47·8	8 49·2	8 23·7	1·1 0·7	7·1 4·2	13·1 7·8
12 8 33·0	8 34·4	8 09·6	1·2 0·7	7·2 4·1	13·2 7·6	12 8 48·0	8 49·4	8 23·9	1·2 0·7	7·2 4·3	13·2 7·8
13 8 33·3	8 34·7	8 09·9	1·3 0·7	7·3 4·2	13·3 7·6	13 8 48·3	8 49·7	8 24·2	1·3 0·8	7·3 4·3	13·3 7·9
14 8 33·5	8 34·9	8 10·1	1·4 0·8	7·4 4·3	13·4 7·7	14 8 48·5	8 49·9	8 24·4	1·4 0·8	7·4 4·4	13·4 7·9
15 8 33·8	8 35·2	8 10·3	1·5 0·9	7·5 4·3	13·5 7·8	15 8 48·8	8 50·2	8 24·7	1·5 0·9	7·5 4·4	13·5 8·0
16 8 34·0	8 35·4	8 10·6	1·6 0·9	7·6 4·4	13·6 7·8	16 8 49·0	8 50·4	8 24·9	1·6 0·9	7·6 4·5	13·6 8·0
17 8 34·3	8 35·7	8 10·8	1·7 1·0	7·7 4·4	13·7 7·9	17 8 49·3	8 50·7	8 25·1	1·7 1·0	7·7 4·6	13·7 8·1
18 8 34·5	8 35·9	8 11·1	1·8 1·0	7·8 4·5	13·8 7·9	18 8 49·5	8 50·9	8 25·4	1·8 1·1	7·8 4·6	13·8 8·2
19 8 34·8	8 36·2	8 11·3	1·9 1·1	7·9 4·5	13·9 8·0	19 8 49·8	8 51·2	8 25·6	1·9 1·1	7·9 4·7	13·9 8·2
20 8 35·0	8 36·4	8 11·5	2·0 1·2	8·0 4·6	14·0 8·1	20 8 50·0	8 51·5	8 25·9	2·0 1·2	8·0 4·7	14·0 8·3
21 8 35·3	8 36·7	8 11·8	2·1 1·2	8·1 4·7	14·1 8·1	21 8 50·3	8 51·7	8 26·1	2·1 1·2	8·1 4·8	14·1 8·3
22 8 35·5	8 36·9	8 12·0	2·2 1·3	8·2 4·7	14·2 8·2	22 8 50·5	8 52·0	8 26·3	2·2 1·3	8·2 4·9	14·2 8·4
23 8 35·8	8 37·2	8 12·3	2·3 1·3	8·3 4·8	14·3 8·2	23 8 50·8	8 52·2	8 26·6	2·3 1·4	8·3 4·9	14·3 8·5
24 8 36·0	8 37·4	8 12·5	2·4 1·4	8·4 4·8	14·4 8·3	24 8 51·0	8 52·5	8 26·8	2·4 1·4	8·4 5·0	14·4 8·5
25 8 36·3	8 37·7	8 12·7	2·5 1·4	8·5 4·9	14·5 8·3	25 8 51·3	8 52·7	8 27·0	2·5 1·5	8·5 5·0	14·5 8·6

Looking at the left hand side of the 34-minute table (above), across the 12-second row, the figure in the "Sun" column shows that the GHA has increased by 8°33′.0.

So at 09:00 the GHA was   316°44′.7
at 09:34:12 it has increased by   8°33′.0
so it has become   325°17′.7

The Sun always goes round the same way, so the GHA correction is always added.

16 | Astro Navigation Handbook

THE CELESTIAL SPHERE

Finding the Declination of the Sun

Finding the Declination of the Sun is a very similar process. Suppose, for instance, that we need to know the Sun's Declination at the same time – 09:34:12 UT on 21 September:-

From the daily page of the almanac, we can see that at 09:00, the Declination was N 0°35'.2, and that it is changing, but very much more slowly than the GHA.

SEPTEMBER 21, 22, 23 (SUN., MON., TUES.)

UT	SUN		MOON				Lat.	Twilight		Sunrise	Moonrise			
	G.H.A.	Dec.	G.H.A.	v	Dec.	d	H.P.		Naut.	Civil		21	22	23	24
	° '	° '	° '	'	° '	'	'	°	h m	h m	h m	h m	h m	h m	h m
21 00	181 42.7	N 0 43.9	47 45.2	7.4	S16 53.3	6.4	59.0	N 72	02 59	04 30	05 39	19 07	18 51	18 39	18 28
01	196 42.9	42.9	62 11.6	7.4	16 46.9	6.5	59.0	N 70	03 19	04 38	05 40	18 36	18 33	18 30	18 27
02	211 43.1	42.0	76 38.0	7.3	16 40.4	6.7	59.0	68	03 34	04 45	05 41	18 14	18 19	18 23	18 25
03	226 43.4	41.0	91 04.3	7.4	16 33.7	6.7	59.1	66	03 47	04 51	05 42	17 56	18 08	18 16	18 24
04	241 43.6	40.0	105 30.7	7.3	16 27.0	6.8	59.1	64	03 57	04 55	05 43	17 41	17 58	18 11	18 23
05	256 43.8	39.1	119 57.0	7.4	16 20.2	7.0	59.2	62	04 05	04 59	05 44	17 29	17 50	18 07	18 22
06	271 44.0	N 0 38.1	134 23.4	7.3	S16 13.2	7.1	59.2	60	04 12	05 03	05 44	17 18	17 42	18 03	18 21
07	286 44.2	37.1	148 49.7	7.3	16 06.1	7.2	59.2	N 58	04 18	05 06	05 45	17 09	17 36	17 59	18 20
08	301 44.5	36.1	163 16.0	7.4	15 58.9	7.3	59.3	56	04 24	05 08	05 45	17 01	17 30	17 56	18 20
S 09	316 44.7	35.2	177 42.4	7.3	15 51.6	7.4	59.3	54	04 28	05 10	05 46	16 54	17 25	17 53	18 19
U 10	331 44.9	34.2	192 08.7	7.3	15 44.2	7.5	59.4	52	04 32	05 12	05 46	16 47	17 21	17 51	18 19
N 11	346 45.1	33.2	206 35.0	7.3	15 36.7	7.6	59.4	50	04 36	05 14	05 46	16 41	17 16	17 48	18 18
D 12	1 45.3	N 0 32.2	221 01.3	7.3	S15 29.1	7.7	59.4	45	04 43	05 18	05 47	16 29	17 07	17 43	18 17
A 13	16 45.6	31.3	235 27.6	7.3	15 21.4	7.9	59.5	N 40	04 49	05 20	05 48	16 18	17 00	17 39	18 16
Y 14	31 45.8	30.3	249 53.9	7.3	15 13.5	7.9	59.5	35	04 53	05 23	05 48	16 09	16 53	17 35	18 15
15	46 46.0	29.3	264 20.2	7.3	15 05.6	8.1	59.5	30	04 57	05 24	05 48	16 01	16 47	17 32	18 15
16	61 46.2	28.4	278 46.5	7.3	14 57.5	8.1	59.6	20	05 01	05 27	05 49	15 47	16 37	17 26	18 14
17	76 46.5	27.4	293 12.8	7.3	14 49.4	8.3	59.6	N 10	05 04	05 28	05 49	15 35	16 29	17 21	18 13
18	91 46.7	N 0 26.4	307 39.1	7.3	S14 41.1	8.4	59.7	0	05 05	05 29	05 49	15 24	16 20	17 16	18 12
19	106 46.9	25.4	322 05.4	7.2	14 32.7	8.4	59.7	S 10	05 04	05 29	05 50	15 13	16 12	17 11	18 11
20	121 47.1	24.5	336 31.6	7.3	14 24.3	8.6	59.7	20	05 02	05 28	05 50	15 01	16 03	17 06	18 10
21	136 47.3	23.5	350 57.9	7.3	14 15.7	8.7	59.8	30	04 58	05 26	05 49	14 47	15 53	17 00	18 09
22	151 47.6	22.5	5 24.2	7.3	14 07.0	8.8	59.8	35	04 55	05 24	05 49	14 39	15 47	16 57	18 08
23	166 47.8	21.5	19 50.5	7.3	13 58.2	8.9	59.8	40	04 51	05 22	05 49	14 30	15 40	16 53	18 07
22 00	181 48.0	N 0 20.6	34 16.8	7.3	S13 49.3	8.9	59.9	45	04 45	05 20	05 49	14 19	15 33	16 49	18 07
01	196 48.2	19.6	48 43.1	7.3	13 40.4	9.1	59.9	S 50	04 39	05 17	05 49	14 06	15 23	16 44	18 06
02	211 48.4	18.6	63 09.4	7.3	13 31.3	9.2	59.9	52	04 35	05 15	05 49	14 00	15 19	16 41	18 05
03	226 48.7	17.7	77 35.7	7.3	13 22.1	9.3	60.0	54	04 31	05 13	05 48	13 53	15 14	16 39	18 05
04	241 48.9	16.7	92 02.0	7.3	13 12.8	9.3	60.0	56	04 27	05 11	05 48	13 46	15 09	16 36	18 04
								58	04 22	05 09	05 48	13 37	15 03	16 32	18 04

This is because the Sun appears to drift up to about 23° north of the Equator in June, and down to S 23 in December. On this particular day, we can see that it has reduced from N0°35'.2 at 09:00 to N0°34'.2 at 10:00.

The hourly rate of change of declination is called "d" and is given at the bottom of the page: in this particular case it is 1'.0 – and so far as the Sun is concerned, that's about the biggest it ever gets.

We could use the **Increments and Corrections** table again. As we are interested in 34 minutes past the hour, we obviously need to look at the 34 minute table, where the right hand side shows that for a v or d value of 1'.0, the appropriate correction is 0'.6.

Astro Navigation Handbook

INCREMENTS AND CORRECTIONS

34m SUN PLANETS	ARIES	MOON	v or Corrn d	v or Corrn d	v or Corrn d	35m SUN PLANETS	ARIES	MOON	v or Corrn d	v or Corrn d	v or Corrn d
s ° ′	° ′	° ′	′ ′	′ ′	′ ′	s ° ′	° ′	° ′	′ ′	′ ′	′ ′
00 8 30·0	8 31·4	8 06·8	0·0 0·0	6·0 3·5	12·0 6·9	00 8 45·0	8 46·4	8 21·1	0·0 0·0	6·0 3·6	12·0 7·1
01 8 30·3	8 31·6	8 07·0	0·1 0·1	6·1 3·5	12·1 7·0	01 8 45·3	8 46·7	8 21·3	0·1 0·1	6·1 3·6	12·1 7·2
02 8 30·5	8 31·9	8 07·2	0·2 0·1	6·2 3·6	12·2 7·0	02 8 45·5	8 46·9	8 21·6	0·2 0·1	6·2 3·7	12·2 7·2
03 8 30·8	8 32·1	8 07·5	0·3 0·2	6·3 3·6	12·3 7·1	03 8 45·8	8 47·2	8 21·8	0·3 0·2	6·3 3·7	12·3 7·3
04 8 31·0	8 32·4	8 07·7	0·4 0·2	6·4 3·7	12·4 7·1	04 8 46·0	8 47·4	8 22·0	0·4 0·2	6·4 3·8	12·4 7·3
05 8 31·3	8 32·6	8 08·0	0·5 0·3	6·5 3·7	12·5 7·2	05 8 46·3	8 47·7	8 22·3	0·5 0·3	6·5 3·8	12·5 7·4
06 8 31·5	8 32·9	8 08·2	0·6 0·3	6·6 3·8	12·6 7·2	06 8 46·5	8 47·9	8 22·5	0·6 0·4	6·6 3·9	12·6 7·5
07 8 31·8	8 33·2	8 08·4	0·7 0·4	6·7 3·9	12·7 7·3	07 8 46·8	8 48·2	8 22·8	0·7 0·4	6·7 4·0	12·7 7·5
08 8 32·0	8 33·4	8 08·7	0·8 0·5	6·8 3·9	12·8 7·4	08 8 47·0	8 48·4	8 23·0	0·8 0·5	6·8 4·0	12·8 7·6
09 8 32·3	8 33·7	8 08·9	0·9 0·5	6·9 4·0	12·9 7·4	09 8 47·3	8 48·7	8 23·2	0·9 0·5	6·9 4·1	12·9 7·6
10 8 32·5	8 33·9	8 09·2	1·0 0·6	7·0 4·0	13·0 7·5	10 8 47·5	8 48·9	8 23·5	1·0 0·6	7·0 4·1	13·0 7·7
11 8 32·8	8 34·2	8 09·4	1·1 0·6	7·1 4·1	13·1 7·5	11 8 47·8	8 49·2	8 23·7	1·1 0·7	7·1 4·2	13·1 7·8
12 8 33·0	8 34·4	8 09·6	1·2 0·7	7·2 4·1	13·2 7·6	12 8 48·0	8 49·4	8 23·9	1·2 0·7	7·2 4·3	13·2 7·8
13 8 33·3	8 34·7	8 09·9	1·3 0·7	7·3 4·2	13·3 7·6	13 8 48·3	8 49·7	8 24·2	1·3 0·8	7·3 4·3	13·3 7·9
14 8 33·5	8 34·9	8 10·1	1·4 0·8	7·4 4·3	13·4 7·7	14 8 48·5	8 49·9	8 24·4	1·4 0·8	7·4 4·4	13·4 7·9
15 8 33·8	8 35·2	8 10·3	1·5 0·9	7·5 4·3	13·5 7·8	15 8 48·8	8 50·2	8 24·7	1·5 0·9	7·5 4·4	13·5 8·0
16 8 34·0	8 35·4	8 10·6	1·6 0·9	7·6 4·4	13·6 7·8	16 8 49·0	8 50·4	8 24·9	1·6 0·9	7·6 4·5	13·6 8·0
17 8 34·3	8 35·7	8 10·8	1·7 1·0	7·7 4·4	13·7 7·9	17 8 49·3	8 50·7	8 25·1	1·7 1·0	7·7 4·6	13·7 8·1
18 8 34·5	8 35·9	8 11·1	1·8 1·0	7·8 4·5	13·8 7·9	18 8 49·5	8 50·9	8 25·4	1·8 1·1	7·8 4·6	13·8 8·2
19 8 34·8	8 36·2	8 11·3	1·9 1·1	7·9 4·5	13·9 8·0	19 8 49·8	8 51·2	8 25·6	1·9 1·1	7·9 4·7	13·9 8·2
20 8 35·0	8 36·4	8 11·5	2·0 1·2	8·0 4·6	14·0 8·1	20 8 50·0	8 51·5	8 25·9	2·0 1·2	8·0 4·7	14·0 8·3
21 8 35·3	8 36·7	8 11·8	2·1 1·2	8·1 4·7	14·1 8·1	21 8 50·3	8 51·7	8 26·1	2·1 1·2	8·1 4·8	14·1 8·3
22 8 35·5	8 36·9	8 12·0	2·2 1·3	8·2 4·7	14·2 8·2	22 8 50·5	8 52·0	8 26·3	2·2 1·3	8·2 4·9	14·2 8·4
23 8 35·8	8 37·2	8 12·3	2·3 1·3	8·3 4·8	14·3 8·2	23 8 50·8	8 52·2	8 26·6	2·3 1·4	8·3 4·9	14·3 8·5
24 8 36·0	8 37·4	8 12·5	2·4 1·4	8·4 4·8	14·4 8·3	24 8 51·0	8 52·5	8 26·8	2·4 1·4	8·4 5·0	14·4 8·5
25 8 36·3	8 37·7	8 12·7	2·5 1·4	8·5 4·9	14·5 8·3	25 8 51·3	8 52·7	8 27·0	2·5 1·5	8·5 5·0	14·5 8·6

In practice, for the Sun, the value of d is so small that it is usually quicker and easier to do it by mental arithmetic: 34 minutes is just over half an hour, so the d correction must be just over half of 1′.0.

At 09:00, the Declination was   N 0°35′.2
at 09:34 it has reduced by   0′.6
so it has become   N 0°34′.6

Remember that the Declination sometimes increases, and sometimes decreases. Be careful to apply the d correction the right way!

Finding the GHA and Declination of other bodies

The process for finding the GHA and Declination of the stars, planets, and moon is similar, but not exactly the same (see pages 52, 44 and 65).

Chapter 4: Time

Imagine, for a moment, that you are taking a traditional visual fix, but that instead of taking a bearing of a lighthouse, you are using some kind of low-flying lightship as your landmark – one that is hurtling westwards at several hundred miles per hour. Timing is obviously critical: if you took the fix a minute later than you thought you did, then the lightship might easily be ten miles further west than you thought, and your fix would be correspondingly wrong as a result.

But that, in effect, is what we are doing when we take and plot an astro fix.

Perhaps it's no wonder, then, that although few people would recognise the name of John Hadley as the inventor of the octant, or John Campbell as the man who developed it into the sextant, many more would know that it was John Harrison who invented the chronometer that earned him the credit for solving "the longitude problem".

That was 250 years ago, and the problem of keeping time is no longer an issue: a £10 quartz watch will easily outperform a traditional chronometer, and regular radio time signals allow us to check it several times a day, anywhere in the world.

But time is still of fundamental importance.

Solar time

The answer to the question "When is noon?" depends to some extent on your definition of "noon" – but it is almost never exactly 12 o'clock!

To an astro navigator, noon means the time at which the Sun crosses their meridian. At this moment the sun is directly south or north of them, and it is as close to their zenith as it is going to get that day.

Remember that the Earth is the centre of the astro universe, so it takes 24 hours for the sun to go once round the Earth, which means that it's moving one degree westwards every four minutes. So if the sun were to cross the Greenwich meridian at 12:00, it wouldn't be noon in Falmouth (5°W) until 12:20.

But there's another snag. In the real universe, the Earth's orbit is neither circular, nor at a constant speed. So the time at which the sun crosses the Greenwich meridian varies – from 16 minutes early in November to 14 minutes late in February!

Astro Navigation Tables tell us whether the sun is running ahead or behind the clock, by telling us the "Equation of Time" or the "Time of Transit" or "Meridian Passage" (they all mean the same).

Universal Time

Universal Time is based on the time at which the sun crosses the meridian that passes through the Greenwich observatory, averaged out over the course of the year. In other words, instead of using the slightly variable movement of the real sun, it is based on the perfectly regular movement of an invisible "mean sun". For that reason, it used to be called "Greenwich Mean Time" or GMT – but that expression has now fallen out of favour, and it is called "Universal Time" (UT) to reflect the fact that it is used as the basis of clock time throughout the world.

> ### UTC
> *The initials UTC stand for Coordinated Universal Time. It's almost the same as UT, but not quite, because while UT is based on the mean sun, UTC is based on atomic clocks.*
>
> *Although we normally think of the world taking 24 hours to spin once, that isn't strictly true: it is slowing down, very slightly, and now takes about two milliseconds longer than 24 hours. Atomic clocks are so accurate that, over a period of about a year and a half, the discrepancy between UT and UTC builds up to almost a second. At that point, an international body called the International Earth Rotation and Reference Systems Service adds a second to UTC – effectively "stopping the clock" for a second, to allow UT to catch up.*

Time Zones

It would be very inconvenient if every town and village kept its own time.

On a global scale, however, it would be equally inconvenient if the whole world were to adopt the same time.

By way of a pragmatic compromise, places in the same general part of the world – such as an entire small or medium-sized country, or a complete state or province – adopt a convenient "standard time". It's usually (but not always) based on UT, offset by a suitable number of whole hours.

The capital of Bermuda, for instance, is Hamilton. It's about 64°47' west of Greenwich, so the sun – moving westwards at 15 degrees per hour – passes Hamilton about 4 hours 19 minutes after it passes Greenwich. So, in keeping with the convention of applying whole-hour adjustments to UT, Bermuda has adopted a standard time that is four hours behind UT.

TIME

CHAPTER 4

Marine time zones

Are an idealised version of the same concept, in which the world is divided into 24 time zones, each shaped roughly like a segment of an orange, and each keeping time one hour ahead or behind its neighbours. Each zone is fifteen degrees across, so the first one, centred on the Prime (Greenwich) Meridian, has its edges at 7°30'W and 7°30'E.

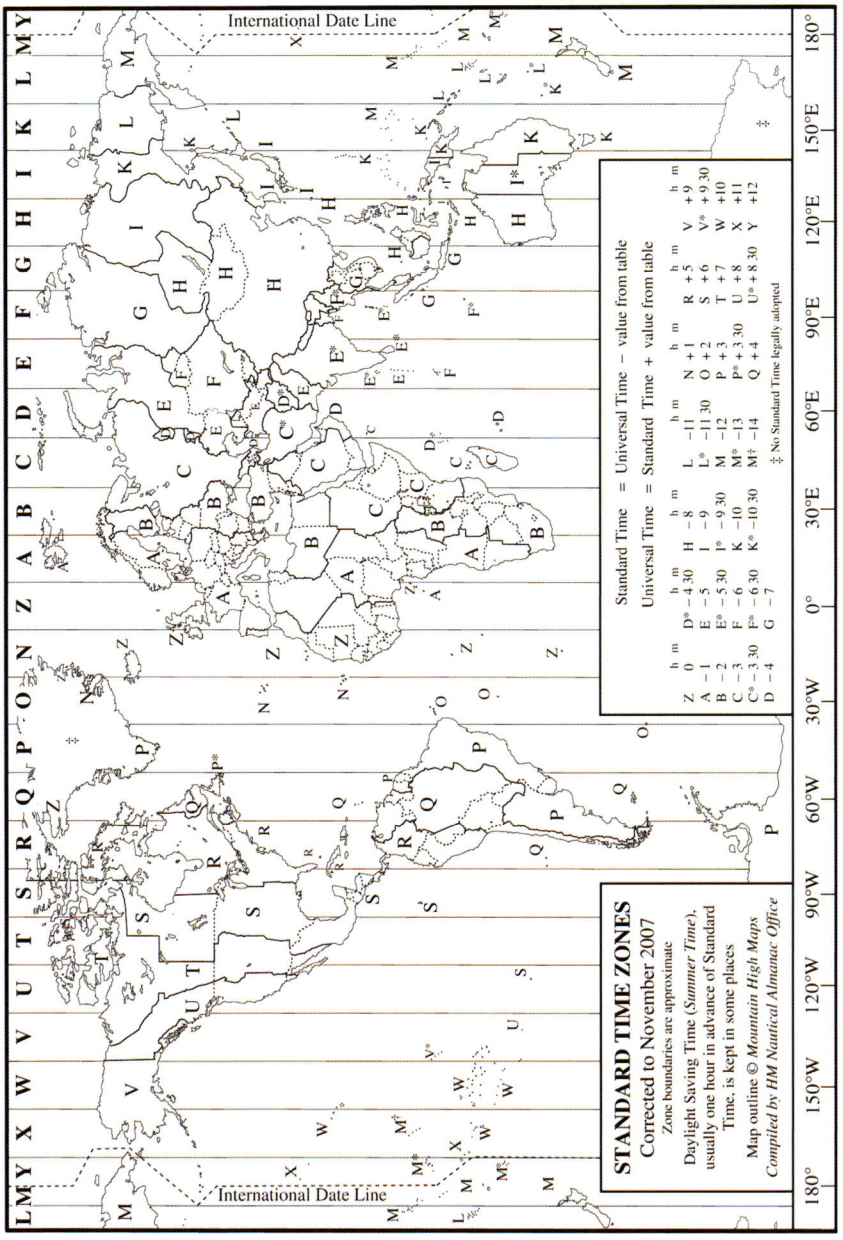

Naming time zones

The simple and obvious way to name time zones is by numbering them: somewhere that differs from UT by one hour could be number one, while somewhere that differs by four hours would be number four, and so on. The only problem would be to differentiate between those that are ahead or behind UT.

In the conventional **nautical system**, used in most technical publications, including those produced by the UK Admiralty, the US Naval Observatory, and Reeds Nautical Almanac:
>	zones that are **ahead of UT (generally those to the east) are designated as negative**
>	zones that are **behind UT (generally those to the west) are designated as positive**

Most of western Europe, for instance, is designated "-1" or "-0100", indicating that you should subtract one hour from the local time to convert from local time to UT.

The **military system** uses letters, rather than numbers.
UT is designated "Z" or "Zulu":
>	zones that are **ahead of UT are designated from A to M (omitting J)**
>	zones that are **behind UT are designated from N to Y**

The **International Standards Organisation** has adopted a system that is the exact opposite of the established nautical system:
>	zones that are **ahead of UT (generally those to the east) are designated as positive**
>	zones that are **behind UT (generally those to the west) are designated as negative**

In this system, most of Europe is designated "+1" or "+0100", indicating that you must add an hour to convert from UT to zone time.

Summer Time

Summer Time, or Daylight Saving Time, is a concept that was developed more or less simultaneously by Britain and Germany during the First World War. The idea was to "save" an hour or so of daylight in the early morning, by putting the clocks forward an hour in spring, and back an hour in autumn.

TIME
CHAPTER 4

CHAPTER 4

When is Noon?

If you were sitting on a beach, or on an anchored boat, you wouldn't need to know the time in order to take a noon sight. You could simply watch the sun as it rises through the morning, then take your sight at the moment it "hangs" in the sky before it starts to fall.

If you're moving, unfortunately things aren't quite that simple. If you were travelling southwards in the northern hemisphere, or northwards in the southern hemisphere, then you would see the sun carry on rising – because you would be getting closer to it – even when a stationary observer at the same spot would see it starting to fall. The problem gets more noticeable at higher speeds, and at twenty or thirty knots, can easily cause position errors of several miles.

For most sailing boat and displacement motor cruiser navigators, though, it is of pretty academic interest: they can either follow the example set by generations of seafarers before the chronometer was invented, and ignore it, or they can calculate when noon will occur and shoot the sun at the right time, regardless of whether it appears to be rising or falling.

The layout and presentation of the data varies between different almanacs, but somewhere within your chosen almanac, you should find something called the "Equation of time" or "Mer.Pass". They effectively mean the same thing, because while the "equation of time" shows the amount by which true Sun leads or lags behind the invisible "mean Sun", "Mer.Pass." shows the time at which the sun crosses the Prime Meridian.

SEPTEMBER 21, 22, 23 (SUN., MON., TUES.)

UT	SUN G.H.A.	Dec.	MOON G.H.A.	v	Dec.	d	H.P.	Lat.	Twilight Naut.	Twilight Civil	Sunrise	Moonrise 21	Moonrise 22	Moonrise 23	Moonrise 24
	° '	° '	° '	'	° '	'	'	°	h m	h m	h m	h m	h m	h m	h m
21 00	181 42.7 N	0 43.9	47 45.2	7.4	S16 53.3	6.4	59.0	N 72	02 59	04 30	05 39	19 07	18 51	18 39	18 28
01	196 42.9	42.9	62 11.6	7.4	16 46.9	6.5	59.0	N 70	03 19	04 38	05 40	18 36	18 33	18 30	18 27
02	211 43.1	42.0	76 38.0	7.3	16 40.4	6.7	59.0	68	03 34	04 45	05 41	18 14	18 19	18 23	18 25
03	226 43.4	41.0	91 04.3	7.4	16 33.7	6.7	59.1	66	03 47	04 51	05 42	17 56	18 08	18 16	18 24
04	241 43.6	40.0	105 30.7	7.3	16 27.0	6.8	59.1	64	03 57	04 55	05 43	17 41	17 58	18 11	18 23
05	256 43.8	39.1	119 57.0	7.4	16 20.2	7.0	59.2	62	04 05	04 59	05 44	17 29	17 50	18 07	18 22
06	271 44.0 N	0 38.1	134 23.4	7.3	S16 13.2	7.1	59.2	60	04 12	05 03	05 44	17 18	17 42	18 03	18 21
07	286 44.2	37.1	148 49.7	7.3	16 06.1	7.2	59.2	N 58	04 18	05 06	05 45	17 09	17 36	17 59	18 20
08	301 44.5	36.1	163 16.0	7.4	15 58.9	7.3	59.3	56	04 24	05 08	05 45	17 01	17 30	17 56	18 20
S 09	316 44.7	35.2	177 42.4	7.3	15 51.6	7.4	59.3	54	04 28	05 10	05 46	16 54	17 25	17 53	18 19
U 10	331 44.9	34.2	192 08.7	7.3	15 44.2	7.5	59.4	52	04 32	05 12	05 46	16 47	17 21	17 51	18 19
		33.2						50	04 36	05 14	05 46	16 41	17 16	17 48	18 18
D 12	1 55.9 S 0	2.2	194 05.9	7.5	S 11.1	11.8	60.9	S 50	17 57	18 30	19 08	04 20	04 57	05 30	06 01
A 13	16 56.1	1.3	208 32.4	7.5	7 29.3	12.0	60.9	52	17 58	18 31	19 11	04 26	05 02	05 34	06 02
Y 14	31 56.4	1.4	222 58.9	7.5	7 37.3	11.9	61.0	54	17 58	18 33	19 15	04 34	05 08	05 37	06 04
15	46 56.6	17.4	237 25.4	7.5	6 55.4	12.1	61.0	56	17 58	18 35	19 20	04 42	05 14	05 41	06 05
16	61 56.8	18.4	251 51.9	7.5	6 43.3	12.0	61.0	58	17 59	18 38	19 25	04 51	05 20	05 45	06 07
17	76 57.0	19.3	266 18.4	7.5	6 31.3	12.2	61.0	S 60	17 59	18 41	19 31	05 01	05 28	05 50	06 09
18	91 57.2 S	20.3	280 44.9	7.5	S 6 19.1	12.1	61.0		SUN			MOON			
19	106 57.4	21.3	295 11.4	7.5	6 07.0	12.3	61.1	Day	Eqn. of Time		Mer.	Mer. Pass.		Age	Phase
20	121 57.7	22.3	309 37.9	7.5	5 54.7	12.2	61.1		00ʰ	12ʰ	Pass.	Upper	Lower		
21	136 57.9	23.2	324 04.4	7.6	5 42.5	12.3	61.1		m s	m s	h m	h m	h m	d	
22	151 58.1	24.2	338 31.0	7.5	5 30.2	12.4	61.1	21	06 50		07 01	21 38	09 10	12	
23	166 58.3	25.2	352 57.5	7.5	5 17.8	12.4	61.1	22	07 12			22 34	10 06	13	○
	S.D. 16.0 d 1.0		S.D. 16.2		16.4		16.6	23	07 33	07 43	11 52	23 29	11 01	14	

24 Astro Navigation Handbook

TIME

Suppose, for instance, we want to find out the time of solar noon on 21 September, in position approximately 42°N 18°W.

From the relevant daily page of the Nautical Almanac, we can see that the equation of time at mid-day on the 21st is 07m 01 secs, and Meridian passage is at 11:53. In other words, the true sun crossed the Prime Meridian seven minutes ahead of the mean sun (see page 20).

Moving westwards at 15 degrees per hour, or taking four minutes to cover one degree, it will cross the 15W meridian an hour later, and will take another twelve minutes to cover the extra three degrees to reach 18W:-

Time of Merpass from Almanac	11 53
Longitude correction (15°W)	+01 00
Longitude correction (3°W)	+00 12
Time of Merpass at 18°W (UT)	13 05

Sunrise, sunset, and twilight

Sunrise, sunset, and twilight are of great significance to the astro navigator, because they are the times at which it is possible to take morning or evening star and planet sights.

Sunrise and sunset are the times at which the upper edge of the Sun first appears or finally disappears below the visible horizon. Atmospheric distortion means that when this occurs the centre of the sun is actually about 1° below the true horizon.

Before sunset or after sunrise, the sky is likely to be too light to see stars, though you may be able to see planets.

Civil and nautical twilight occur when the sun is six degrees and twelve degrees below the horizon. When the sun is more than twelve degrees below the horizon, the horizon is likely to be too indistinct to take star sights. Ideally, star sights should be taken between morning civil twilight and sunrise, and between sunset and evening civil twilight.

The procedures for finding the times of sunrise, sunset, and twilight are almost identical, using the data given in the daily pages of the Nautical Almanac.

TIME

CHAPTER 4

SEPTEMBER 21, 22, 23 (SUN., MON., TUES.)

UT	SUN G.H.A.	SUN Dec.	MOON G.H.A.	MOON v	MOON Dec.	MOON d	MOON H.P.	Lat.	Twilight Naut.	Twilight Civil	Sunrise	Moonrise 21	Moonrise 22	Moonrise 23	Moonrise 24
21 00	181 42.7	N 0 43.9	47 45.2	7.4	S16 53.3	6.4	59.0	N 72	02 59	04 30	05 39	19 07	18 51	18 39	18 28
01	196 42.9	42.9	62 11.6	7.4	16 46.9	6.5	59.0	N 70	03 19	04 38	05 40	18 36	18 33	18 30	18 27
		42.0						68	03 34	04 45	05 41	18 14	18 19	18 23	18 25
		41.0											15 08		
04	241 46.9		92 02.0	7.3	13 12.6	9.3	60.0	58	04 22	05 07	05 48	13 57	15 03	16 32	18 04
05	256 49.1	1.0	106 28.3	7.3	13 03.5	9.5	60.1	S 60	04 17	05 06	05 48	13 28	14 56	16 29	18 03
06	271 49.3	N 0 14	120 54.6	7.3	S12 54.0	9.6	60.1	Lat.	Sunset	Twilight Civil	Twilight Naut.	Moonset 21	Moonset 22	Moonset 23	Moonset 24
07	286 49.5	13.8	135 20.9	7.3	12 44.4	9.8	60.1								
08	301 49.8	12.8	149 47.2	7.3	12 34.8	9.8	60.2								
M 09	316 50.0	.. 11.8	164 13.5	7.3	12 25.0	9.8	60.2								
O 10	331 50.2	10.8	178 39.8	7.3	12 15.2	9.9	60.2	°	h m	h m	h m	h m	h m	h m	h m
N 11	346 50.4	09.9	193 06.1	7.3	12 05.3	10.0	60.2	N 72	18 04	19 12	20 42	24 25	00 25	02 39	04 48
D 12	1 50.6	N 0 08.9	207 32.4	7.4	S11 55.3	10.1	60.3	N 70	18 03	19 04	20 22	24 54	00 54	02 54	04 54
A 13	16 50.9	07.9	221 58.8	7.3	11 45.2	10.2	60.3	68	18 02	18 58	20 08	25 16	01 16	03 07	04 59
Y 14	31 51.1	07.0	236 25.1	7.3	11 35.0	10.3	60.3	66	18 01	18 52	19 56	25 33	01 33	03 17	05 03
15	46 51.3	.. 06.0	250 51.4	7.4	11 24.7	10.4	60.4	64	18 01	18 48	19 46	00 14	01 47	03 25	05 07
16	61 51.5	05.0	265 17.8	7.3	11 14.3	10.4	60.4	62	18 00	18 44	19 38	00 30	01 58	03 33	05 10
17	76 51.7	04.0	279 44.1	7.4	11 03.9	10.6	60.4	60	18 00	18 41	19 31	00 43	02 08	03 39	05 13
18	91 52.0	N 0 03.1	294 10.5	7.3	S10 53.3	10.6	60.5	N 58	17 59	18 38	19 25	00 54	02 16	03 44	05 15
19	106 52.2	02.1	308 36.8	7.4	10 42.7	10.7	60.5	56	17 59	18 36	19 20	01 04	02 24	03 49	05 17
20	121 52.4	01.1	323 03.2	7.4	10 32.0	10.7	60.5	54	17 58	18 34	19 16	01 13	02 30	03 53	05 19
21	136 52.6	N 0 00.1	337 29.6	7.4	10 21.3	10.9	60.6	52	17 58	18 32	19 12	01 20	02 36	03 57	05 21
22	151 52.8	S 0 00.8	351 56.0	7.4	10 10.4	10.9	60.6	50	17 58	18 30	19 08	01 27	02 42	04 01	05 22
23	166 53.1	01.8	6 22.4	7.3	9 59.5	11.0	60.6	45	17 57	18 27	19 01	01 42	02 53	04 08	05 26
23 00	181 53.3	S 0 02.8	20 48.7	7.4	S 9 48.5	11.1	60.6	N 40	17 57	18 24	18 56	01 54	03 03	04 15	05 28
01	196 53.5	03.8	35 15.1	7.4	9 37.4	11.1	60.7	35	17 57	18 22	18 51	02 04	03 11	04 20	05 31
02	211 53.7	04.7	49 41.5	7.5	9 26.3	11.2	60.7	30	17 57	18 20	18 48	02 13	03 18	04 25	05 33
03	226 53.9	.. 05.7	64 08.0	7.4	9 15.1	11.3	60.7	20	17 56	18 18	18 44	02 29	03 30	04 33	05 36
04	241 54.2	06.7	78 34.4	7.4	9 03.8	11.4	60.7	N 10	17 56	18 17	18 41	02 42	03 41	04 40	05 40
05	256 54.4	07.6	93 00.8	7.4	8 52.4	11.4	60.8	0	17 56	18 17	18 41	02 55	03 51	04 47	05 42

Suppose, for instance, we want to find out the time of civil twilight in the evening of 21 September, in position approximately 42°N 18°W.

From the daily page of the Almanac, we can see that civil twilight at a latitude of 40°N is at 18 24, and at 45°N it is at 18 27. It's easy to see that for the latitude we are interested in (42°) the time must be somewhere between these two: call it 18 25.

Strictly speaking, this only applies to the middle day of the three days covered by this page of the almanac, but in practice the times change very little from one day to the next.

This, however, is the time of Civil Twilight on the Prime Meridian: it still has to be corrected for Longitude, using exactly the same technique as for the time of noon.

Time of Twilight from Almanac	18 25
Longitude correction (15W)	+01 00
Longitude correction (3W)	+00 12
Time of Twilight at 42N 18W (UT)	19 37

Astro Navigation Handbook | 27

Chapter 5: The Noon Sight

There has always been something special about the noon sight. Until chronometers started to become widespread, the noon sight was one of very few sources of position information that was available to seafarers out of sight of land.

Unfortunately, because it is based on a single body, a noon sight can only provide a single position line (just like a visual bearing of a single landmark), but it is still important because it is one of the easiest sights to understand, to take, and to plot.

What makes it so special is that just for a moment, at "local noon", the sun, the observer, and the north and south poles all lie in the same plane – which means that we can visualise the situation with a two-dimensional diagram, and work out the angles involved by simple arithmetic.

Taking the sight

In the particular case of a noon sight, slow boat navigators don't need to worry about precise timing, though it's useful to have a rough idea of when it is likely to occur. (See page 24.)

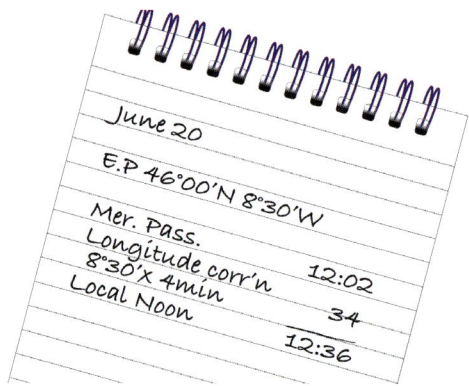

A few minutes before the expected time, settle yourself in a suitable spot, check and adjust the sextant for errors, and take a practice sight, but don't re-set the sextant to zero.

Look through the sextant again, a minute or so later, and you should see the reflected image of the sun lifting away from the horizon. Tweak the micrometer to bring it back down, then wait another minute or so before repeating the process.

Eventually, instead of rising, the sun will start to fall, and you will see the reflected image starting to dip into the horizon. This is the time to read the sextant.

> Whatever you do, don't be tempted to tweak the micrometer to push the reflected image back up to the horizon!

The last reading on the sextant before the sun started to fall is the Sextant Altitude of the sun as it crossed the meridian.

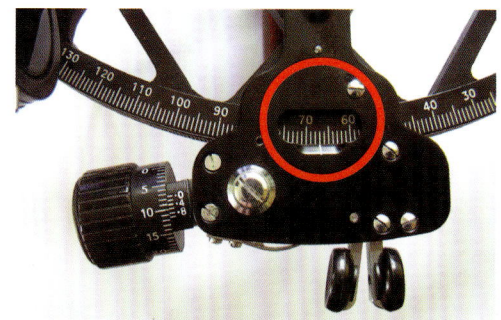

In the photograph, for instance, the reading is 67°07'.5.

THE NOON SIGHT
CHAPTER 5

The geometry

We don't really want to know how high the Sun is above the horizon: what is much more interesting is how far it is from our Zenith – the point directly overhead. But it's easy to find the Zenith Distance by subtracting the Altitude from 90°.

Zenith Distance = 90 - Altitude

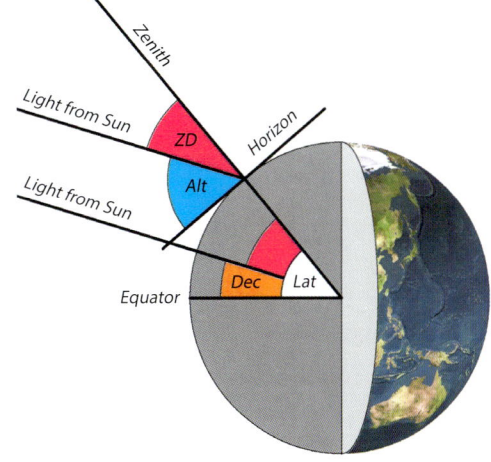

The diagram shows that during the summer months – when the observer and the Sun are both on the same side of the Equator,

Zenith Distance + Declination = Latitude

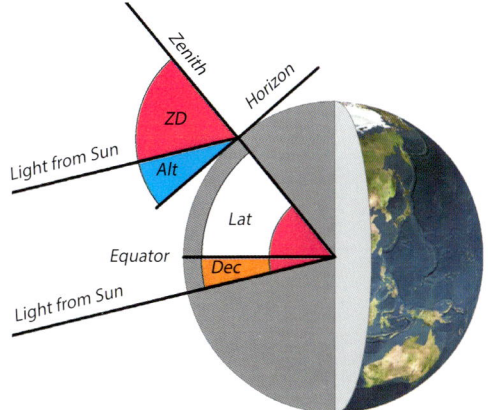

In winter the geometry changes, and the formula becomes:

Zenith Distance - Declination = Latitude

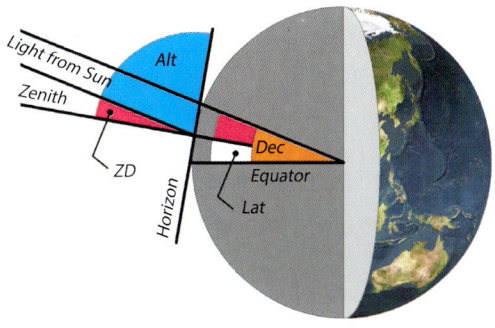

There's a bit of an oddball situation in the tropical summer, where your latitude may be less than the declination of the Sun. The formula for that is:

Declination - Zenith Distance = Latitude

Astro Navigation Handbook

CHAPTER 5

And the arithmetic

The arithmetic is mostly concerned with small corrections, intended to make the end result as accurate as possible.

The Sextant Altitude, in particular, needs to be corrected for five errors:

Index error: the residual error in the sextant after it has been adjusted

Dip: an error that depends on your height of eye above the waterline, caused by the fact that if you are above the waterline, your line of sight to the visible horizon must be angled very slightly downwards

Refraction: an error of between zero and 6', caused by the sun's rays being refracted (bent) when they pass through our atmosphere

Semi-diameter: an error of about 16', caused by measuring the altitude of the bottom of the sun, rather than the middle of it

Parallax: an error of between zero and 0'.12, caused by the fact that the sun is not really on the inner surface of an infinitely distant celestial sphere! It is effectively negligible

The Index error is found by checking the sextant (see page 12), but the others are all found in The Nautical Almanac or its civilian counterparts.

ALTITUDE CORRECTION TABLES 10°–90°—SUN, STARS, PLANETS

OCT.–MAR. SUN APR.–SEPT.						STARS AND PLANETS			DIP				
App. Alt.	Lower Limb	Upper Limb	App. Alt.	Lower Limb	Upper Limb	App. Alt.	Corrⁿ	App. Alt.	Additional Corrⁿ	Ht. of Eye	Corrⁿ	Ht. of Eye	Ht. of Eye Corrⁿ
° '			° '			° '			1980	m		ft.	m '
9 34	+10·8	−21·5	9 39	+10·6	−21·2	9 56	−5·3		VENUS	2·4	−2·8	8·0	1·0 − 1·8
9 45	+10·9	−21·4	9 51	+10·7	−21·1	10 08	−5·2		Jan. 1-Feb. 26	2·6	−2·9	8·6	1·5 − 2·2
9 56	+11·0	−21·3	10 03	+10·8	−21·0	10 20	−5·1	°		2·8	−3·0	9·2	2·0 − 2·5
10 08			10 15	+10·9	−20·9	10 33	−5·0	42	+ 0·1	3·0	−3·1	9·8	2·5 − 2·8
		17	10 27	+11·0	−20·8	10 46	−4·9			3·2		10·5	3·0 − 3·0
43 59	+15·2	−17·1	10 40			11 00	−4·8		Feb. 27-Apr. 13	3·4	−3·2	11·2	See table
47 10	+15·3	−17·0									−3·3	11·9	←
50 46	+15·4	−16·9	52 44	+15·2	−16·6	56 11	−0·7		MARS	17·9		12·6	m
54 49	+15·5	−16·8	57 02	+15·3	−16·5	60 28	−0·6		Jan. 1-Apr. 28	18·4	−7·5	13	
59 23	+15·6	−16·7	61 51	+15·4	−16·4	65 08	−0·5	°		18·8	−7·6	2·1	130 − 11·1
64 30	+15·7	−16·6	67 17	+15·5	−16·3	70 11	−0·4	41	+ 0·2	19·3	−7·7	63·8	135 − 11·3
70 12	+15·8	−16·5	73 16	+15·6	−16·2	75 34	−0·3	75	+ 0·1	19·8	−7·8	65·4	140 − 11·5
76 26	+15·9	−16·4	79 43	+15·7	−16·1	81 13	−0·2		Apr. 29-Dec. 31	20·4	−7·9	67·1	145 − 11·7
83 05	+16·0	−16·3	86 32	+15·8	−16·0	87 03	−0·1	°		20·9	−8·0	68·8	150 − 11·9
90 00	+16·1	−16·2	90 00	+15·9	−15·9	90 00	0·0	60	+ 0·1	21·4	−8·1	70·5	155 − 12·1

App. Alt. = Apparent altitude = Sextant altitude corrected for index error and dip.

Astro Navigation Handbook

THE NOON SIGHT

CHAPTER 5

Suppose, for instance, that we are on passage from the English Channel to the Med, on 20 June, and our position is approximately 46°N 8°30'W. At about 1236UT, the greatest altitude of the Sun's lower limb is measured as 67°07'.5, taken with the sextant 3.2 m above the waterline, and an index error of 5'.3 on the arc:

1. Correct for Index error
In this case, the error is "on" the arc, so it must be taken off

Sextant Altitude	67°07'.5
Index error	- 5'.3
Observed Altitude	67°02'.2

2. Correct for Dip
The correction for Dip is found in the corrections page of the Nautical Almanac. It must always be subtracted

Observed Altitude	67°02'.2
Correction for Dip	- 3'.1
Apparent Altitude	66°59'.1

3. Correct for Refraction, Semi-diameter, and Parallax
The corrections for all three of these are combined in one table, also found on the corrections page of the Nautical Almanac. Assuming that you have measured the altitude of the bottom edge of the sun, the centre of the sun must be higher, by half the sun's apparent diameter. This "semi-diameter" varies slightly during the year, so the table is in two parts:

Apparent Altitude	66°59'.1
Correction SD etc.	+ 15'.5
True Altitude	67°14'.6

4. Find the True Zenith Distance
Subtract the True Altitude from ninety degrees

	90°00'.0
True Altitude	- 67°14'.6
True Zenith Distance	22°45'.4

5. Find the Declination of the Sun
The Sun's declination is found from the daily page of the Almanac (see page 15).
In this case, it is N23°26′.3.

6. Calculate your latitude
Use the appropriate seasonal formula to combine the Sun's Declination and its True Zenith Distance to find your latitude. In this case, in June, it is summer, so the appropriate formula (from page 29) is:
Zenith Distance + Declination = Latitude

Zenith Distance	22°45′.4
Declination	+ N23°26′.3
Latitude	46°11′.7N

The answer can be plotted straight onto the navigational chart as an east-west line, or written into the log book.

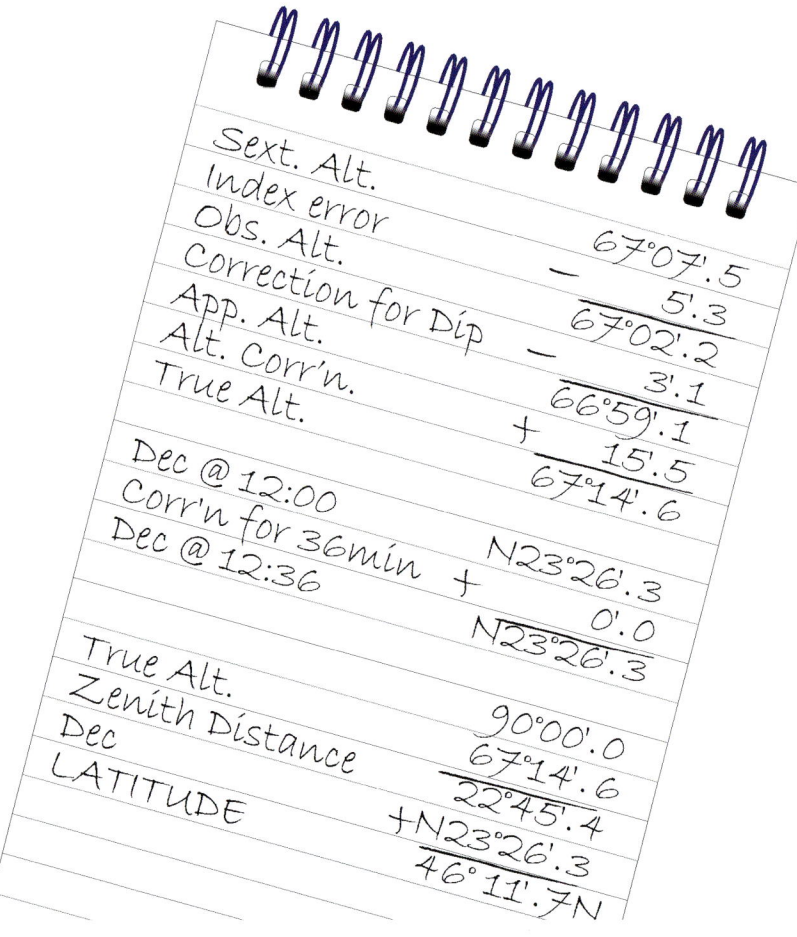

Chapter 6: Morning And Afternoon Sun Sights

Most navigators are quite familiar with the idea that a minute of latitude is one sea mile. So it is reasonably obvious that in a noon sight, the Zenith Distance corresponds directly to the distance between your own position and the spot at which the sun is directly overhead.

In the example in the previous chapter, for instance:
    the latitude of the spot at which the sun was directly overhead was 23°26′.3N
    the zenith distance was 22°45′.4
    so the latitude of the observer was 46°11′.7N

It would be rather a convoluted way of doing it, but we could – at least in theory – have achieved the same result by converting the zenith distance to minutes of arc (22°45′.4 =1365′.4) and then measuring 1365.4 sea miles northwards from 23°26′.3 N.

Still thinking "in theory" there is no reason why this idea should not apply just as well when the sun is somewhere other than directly north or south of us. After all, the Earth is very nearly spherical*, so there is no reason why the basic geometry should change if we took a sight when the sun was in any other direction.

One big practical problem with this is that most sights involve huge distances – anything up to five thousand miles – so it is almost impossible to plot them accurately on paper charts.

There are various ways round this problem, but one, in particular, stands out. It's known as the Marcq St Hilaire method, named after the French captain who invented it in the late nineteenth century.

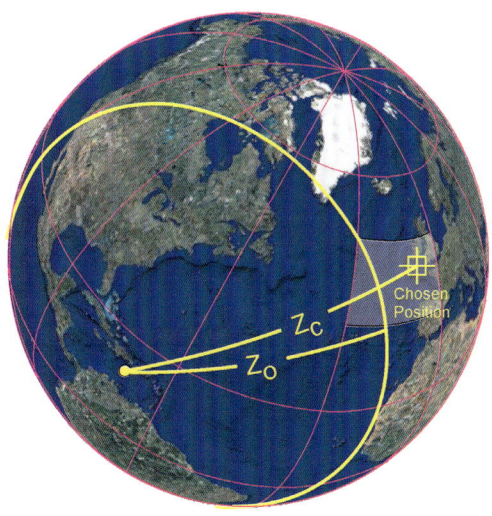

The reasoning behind St Hilaire's method is that your position lies somewhere on the circumference of a circle, whose radius corresponds to the True Zenith Distance and whose centre is the point at which the sun is directly overhead. If you choose some arbitrary point, and work out what the Zenith Distance would have been if you were seeing it from your chosen position, then the difference between the True Zenith Distance (Z_o) and the Calculated Zenith Distance (Z_c) is a measure of the distance between your chosen position and your position circle, called the *intercept*.

The beauty of this is that it doesn't call for a chart showing half the world. If we pick our chosen position wisely, the whole thing can easily be done on an A4 sheet of paper. Nor do you need to be as clever a mathematician as St Hilaire, because all the trigonometry involved has already been done, and

*The earth is not a perfect sphere: it is slightly flattened at the poles. But the distortion is only about a third of one percent, so for practical purposes it can be ignored.

Astro Navigation Handbook | 33

the answers published in books of pre-calculated **Sight Reduction Tables**. All we have to know is how to extract the right answer from the book!

Sight Reduction Tables are available from various sources, but generally fall into two categories:
- Sight Reduction Tables for Marine Navigation are versatile and offer a higher level of precision, but they are bulky and time-consuming to use.
- Sight Reduction Tables for Air Navigation are almost completely redundant for their original purpose, but are ideal for use on yachts and small ships.

The PZX triangle

The key to Marcq St Hilaire's method is what generations of seafarers have come to know as the PZX triangle:-
- P represents the nearest celestial Pole,
- Z represents the Zenith at the chosen position, and
- X represents the position of a heavenly body such as the Sun.

As we're dealing with angles, rather than miles or metres, it really doesn't matter if you prefer to scale the whole thing down and think of P as the nearest Pole, Z as the chosen position, and X as the position at which the heavenly body is overhead.

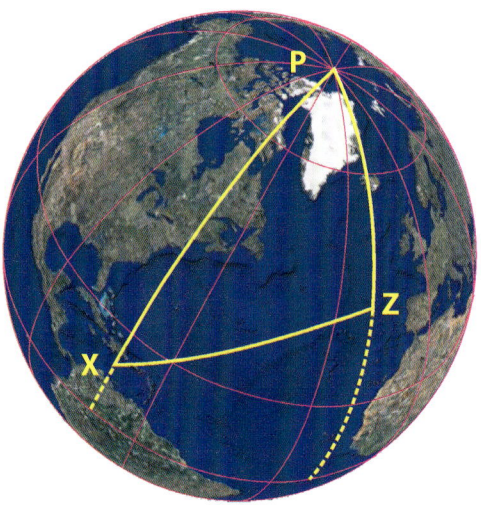

These three make up the corners of a huge triangle, in which ZX is the side we are interested in: we want to know its length (expressed in degrees and minutes) and – for reasons which will soon be obvious – its direction.

Fortunately, we already have some information about this triangle:

- side PX = 90°- Declination of X
- side PZ = 90°- Latitude of Z and
- the angle at P = GHA of X - Longitude of Z

The Local Hour Angle (LHA)

The last of these – "the angle at P" – is known as the **Local Hour Angle**.

Just as the Greenwich Hour Angle is the angular distance of a heavenly body west of the Greenwich Meridian, the LHA is its angular distance west of the local meridian.

MORNING AND AFTERNOON SUN SIGHTS

CHAPTER 6

Working out the LHA is a matter of simple addition or subtraction, especially as we are usually concerned with whole degrees, but it is important to be aware of the fact that the GHA is always measured Westwards, while longitude is measured eastwards or westwards.

Suppose, for instance, that a yacht is at 8°30′W, and the GHA of the Sun is 70°.
The Local Hour Angle (LHA) is 70°- 8°30′W = 61°30′

Now suppose the yacht is at 8°30′E, and the GHA of the Sun is 70°.
Now, the LHA is 70°+8°30′E = 78°30′

The magic formulae

If PZX were an ordinary, flat, two-dimensional triangle, knowing three things about it would be enough to let us calculate all the other lengths and angles. Being a triangle on the surface of a sphere makes the trigonometry more complicated, but the principle is precisely the same: knowing the length of two sides and the angle between them is enough to calculate the length of the missing side and angles.

The important bit, so far as astro navigation is concerned, boils down to two remarkably simple formulae:
- To find the Calculated Altitude (H_c):
  $\sin H_c = \cos \text{Lat} \times \cos \text{Dec} \times \cos \text{LHA} \pm \sin \text{Lat} \times \sin \text{Dec}$
  The "±" is an addition sign if Lat and Dec are in the same hemisphere as each other, and a subtraction sign if they are in different hemispheres.

- To find the Azimuth (direction)
  $\sin Z = (\sin \text{LHA} \times \cos \text{Dec}) / \cos H_c$

Air Sight Reduction Tables

There is an infinite number of possible PZX triangles that could be drawn on the surface of the Earth, each with a different Latitude and Longitude for Z, and a different Declination and GHA for X. No book of tables could possibly give answers for all of them.

We're dealing with an arbitrary chosen position, so one obvious way to simplify things is to use whole degrees, rather than messing about with minutes and fractions.

Suppose, for instance, that we are on passage from the English Channel to the Med, on 20 June, and that our estimated position at 1800UT is 45°38′.8N 8°30′W. At about 1830UT, a series of sun sights are taken: the average time is 18:28:08 UT and the average sextant altitude of the Sun's lower limb is 17°41′.2. The sextant 2.0 m above the waterline, and its index error is 5′.3 on the arc:

CHAPTER 6

The first stage in the process is to refer to the Almanac, to correct the Sextant Altitude for its various errors:-

Sextant Altitude	17°41'.2
Index error	- 5'.3
Observed Altitude	17°35'.9
Correction for Dip	- 2'.5
Apparent Altitude	17°33'.4
Correction for SD etc.	+ 13'.0
True Altitude	17°46'.4

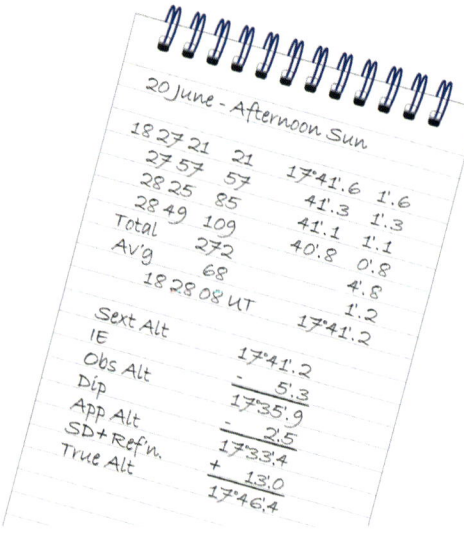

Still referring to the Almanac, we need to find the GHA and Declination of the Sun at the time of the sight:-

GHA at 18:00	89°36'.3
inc. for 28m 08s	+ 7°02'.0
GHA at 18:28:08	96°38'.3
Dec at 18:00	N 23°26'.3
inc. for 28m 08s	+ 0'.0
Dec at 18:28:08	N 23°26'.3

Now we need to choose a position, somewhere in the vicinity of the EP, but which will give a whole number of degrees for its latitude and Local Hour Angle.

The latitude is easy: the nearest whole number of degrees to the EP (45°38'.8N) is 46N.

The Local Hour Angle is simple arithmetic: our Longitude is 8°30'W, and the Sun's GHA is 96° 38'.3. We are looking for a longitude close to 8°30'W, which will leave a whole number of degrees when it is subtracted from 96°38'.3.

GHA at 18:28:08	96°38'.3
Chosen Longitude	08°38'.3
LHA	88°

Astro Navigation Handbook

MORNING AND AFTERNOON SUN SIGHTS

CHAPTER 6

Now, at last, we are ready to go into the Sight Reduction Tables:

- First, find the volume that includes our chosen latitude
- Then find the half dozen pages that cover our chosen latitude
- Within that group, find the couple of pages that cover the correct declination – note that the declination may be the "same" as the latitude or "contrary"
- Finally, find the specific page that covers our LHA

Probably the commonest single mistake in astro navigation is to look at the wrong page of the sight reduction tables – particularly to look at the "same declination" instead of the "contrary declination", or vice versa. On that page find the column that corresponds to the Declination and the row that corresponds to our LHA. At that point, there is a group of three figures: labels at the top of the column tell us that they are H_c, d, and Z, and in this particular example they are: 17°40, 41, and 75.

H_c and Z are the calculated Altitude and Azimuth, for our chosen position, but for a body whose declination was N23, rather than N23°26'.3.

d is an indication of how a change in declination would affect the Altitude. In this case, for instance, d=41, meaning that the Altitude would be 41mins greater if the declination was increased by one degree.

To make the correction, we need to look for the "Correction to Tabulated Altitude for Minutes of Declination" Table in the Sight Reduction Tables, finding the row that corresponds to the minutes of Declination and the column that corresponds to the value of d that we found in the main table. In this particular case, the answer is +18', which has to be added to the tabulated H_c:

H_c	17°40'	(d=+41)
Corr'n for minutes of Dec	18'	
H_c	17°58'	

Astro Navigation Handbook 37

TABLE 5. — Correction to Tabulated Altitude for Minutes of Declination

[Table 5 image showing correction values for declination minutes 1-46 across rows 0-30, with row 26 and column 41 highlighted in red]

Z also needs converting. We would like it to be the true bearing of the Sun – the direction ZX in diagram on page 34. But in fact, it is the angle Z – which isn't quite the same thing. In the corners of the pages of the Sight Reduction Tables, there are notes about converting "Z" to a true bearing:

N. Lat LHA greater than 180°.......Z_n=Z
      LHA less than 180°...............Z_n=360°-Z

S. Lat LHA greater than 180°.......Z_n=180°-Z
      LHA less than 180°.............Z_n=180°+Z

So in this case, with a northerly latitude and an LHA of less than 180,
Z_n=360°-Z :- 360°-75° = 285°

Azimuth and Intercept

It's all too easy, when you're in the thick of tables and calculations, to lose sight of your real objective. Remember that the whole point of all this mathematical jiggery-pokery is to draw a section of a huge position circle on the chart or plotting sheet.

To do that, we need to know whether the chosen position is inside or outside the position circle, and by how far.

So the final stage of the maths is to take the True Altitude (often called H_o) away from the Calculated Altitude (H_c) – or vice versa.

H_c	17°58′.0
H_o	17°46′.4
Intercept	11′.6

38 Astro Navigation Handbook

MORNING AND AFTERNOON SUN SIGHTS

To plot the position line on a chart or plotting sheet, the first step is to mark the chosen position.

Next, draw a line through the Chosen Position indicating the Sun's Azimuth, or bearing, and measure off the intercept along it – making sure that you measure in the right direction.

- **If H_o is smaller than H_c, the true position must be further from the Sun than the Chosen Position.**

- **If H_o is larger than H_c, the true position must be closer to the Sun than the Chosen Position.**

You may find the mnemonic "Tiny Tab Towards" helpful, as a reminder that if the Tabulated Altitude is tinier, then the position line is closer towards the heavenly body.

In this particular example, the Azimuth (found from the Sight Reduction Tables) is 285° but H_o is smaller than H_c, so the intercept has to be drawn and measured in the opposite direction – 105°.

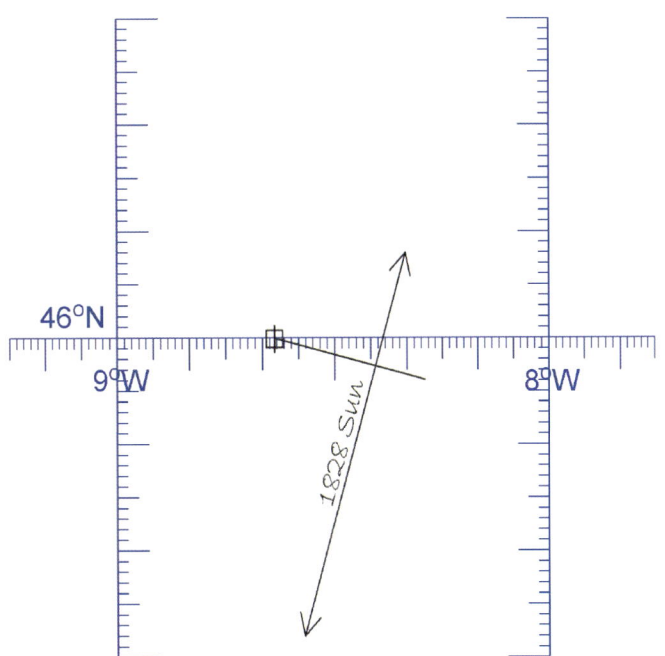

What we've drawn is, in effect, a tiny section of the position circle, with the end of the intercept representing just one of the infinite number of possible positions that lie somewhere on its circumference. The position circle is so huge that we can easily represent the short section of its circumference that is of interest to us by a straight line, at right angles to the intercept.

CHAPTER 6

A coastal navigator, faced with just one object from which to obtain a visual fix, might well choose to use a running fix. An ocean navigator, with just one Sun, can use exactly the same technique, crossing the position line from an afternoon sun sight with a transferred position line from an earlier sun sight – such as their noon latitude.

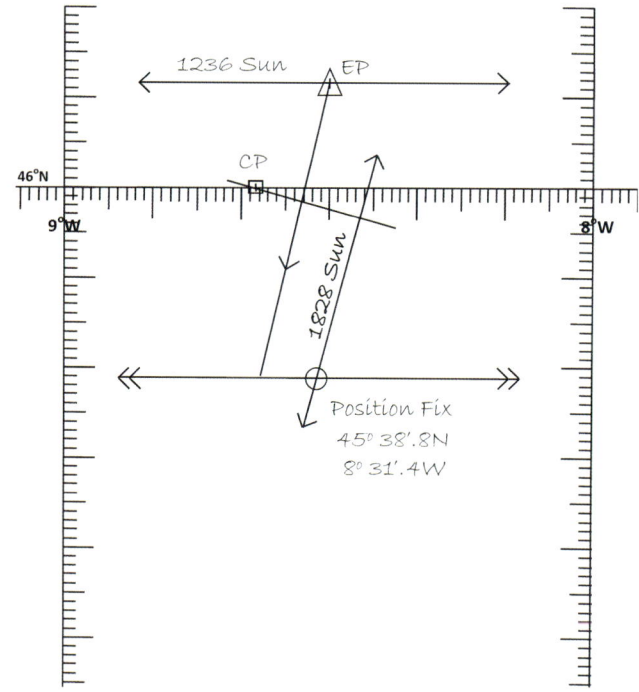

Running fix

Suppose you've taken a bearing of a lighthouse, but for some reason or other, you have not been able to cross it with another position line in order to produce a fix.

Some time later, the boat has moved on.

If you had been starting with a fix, you'd be able to work out an estimated position. But you don't: you only know that you were somewhere along the line ABC.

40 | Astro Navigation Handbook

MORNING AND AFTERNOON SUN SIGHTS

If you had been at A, your EP would be at D; if you had been at B, your EP would be at E, and if you had been at C, your EP would be at F.

D, E, and F all lie on a straight line, parallel to the original position line, but separated from it by the direction and distance the boat has moved since the original bearing was taken.

The line DEF is called a transferred position line, and once you've worked it out, it can be treated like any other position line, and crossed with any other position line to produce a running fix.

You don't, in practice, have to work on several points along the original position line. One is enough, and it can be anywhere – though it is usual to choose the spot that is closest to where you believe yourself to be.

Sight reduction by calculator

Sight reduction tables are nothing more than books of pre-calculated solutions of mathematical formulae.

Before they became popular, it was quite normal for navigators to carry out the calculations themselves, using log tables (logarithms) to take some of the effort and error out of the long division and long multiplication involved.

Nowadays, of course, log tables and slide rules are history – their place taken by pocket calculators, PDAs, and PCs.

There are many different computer and PDA programmes available, both commercially and as freeware, and many different formulae available that can be used with pocket calculators.

One widely used set of formulae are:-

To find H_c if Lat and Dec have the same name
H_c = Inv sin (cos Lat x cos Dec x cos LHA + sin Lat x sin Dec)

To find H_c if Lat and Dec have different names
H_c = Inv sin (cos Lat x cos Dec x cos LHA - sin Lat x sin Dec)

To find Azimuth
$$Z = \text{Invsin} \left(\frac{\sin \text{LHA} \times \cos \text{Dec}}{\cos H_c} \right)$$

Note that the azimuth calculation gives the direction in quadrantal notation – i.e. degrees from North or South. So an answer of 075 (for instance) could mean 075°, 105°, 255°, or 285°.

The easiest way to resolve the ambiguity is to take a compass bearing of the heavenly body.

CHAPTER 6

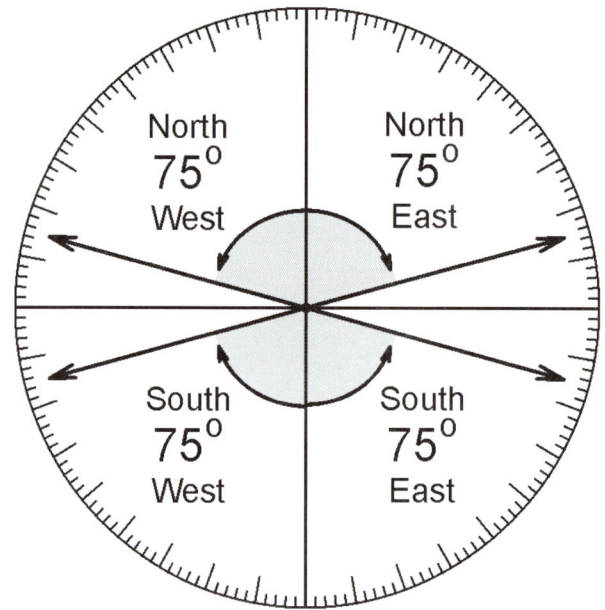

Compass check by sun

As an integral part of the process of finding the position line, this calculation – whether by sight reduction tables or by calculator – has given us the true bearing of the Sun.

This, of course, can be used as a means of checking the compass: many compasses are even fitted with a shadow pin, sticking straight upwards from the centre of the card for that very purpose.

If you just want a compass check, you don't have to go through the whole calculation: the sextant altitude and its associated corrections are irrelevant, and the calculation of LHA and Declination can be rounded off to the nearest whole degree.

Chapter 7:   Planets

As a means of fixing position, the Sun may be blindingly obvious, but it has one major drawback....

There is only one of it!

This means that we can only ever get one position line from it at a time – never a complete fix in one go. So although many ocean passages have been made without using anything other than the Sun, there are good reasons for looking at some of the other bodies available.

The Moon appears to be just as big as the Sun, and is often just as obvious, but for a variety of reasons, moon sights are more difficult to take and to calculate than most.

The next brightest thing in the sky is Venus: it's often visible even in daylight, and is almost always either the first "star" to appear at dusk or the last to fade at dawn. Jupiter isn't quite as bright, but it still outshines the brightest of the true stars. Mars and Saturn aren't as outstanding as Venus and Jupiter, but they are still comparable with the brightest stars. All four share an important advantage for astro navigators:-

- The techniques and reference books that you use for planet sights are almost identical to those that apply to the Sun. The only differences are an extra step in the process of finding the GHA, and the use of a different table for correcting the Sextant Altitude.

CHAPTER 7

Finding the Greenwich Hour Angle and Declination of a planet

Data for the stars and planets are published in The Nautical Almanac, and in civilian publications such as Reeds Astro Navigation Tables.

JUNE 20, 21, 22 (FRI., SAT., SUN.)

UT	ARIES G.H.A.	VENUS −3.2 G.H.A.	Dec.	MARS +1.1 G.H.A.	Dec.	JUPITER −1.5 G.H.A.	Dec.	SATURN +1.3 G.H.A.	Dec.	STARS Name	S.H.A.	Dec.
20 00	268 21.4	187 29.4	N20 56.8	98 10.4	N 5 03.9	111 41.1	N10 55.7	95 51.9	N 5 38.5	Acamar	315 37.7	S40 22.9
01	283 23.9	202 33.4	56.2	113 11.7	03.4	126 43.2	55.6	110 54.2	38.4	Achernar	335 45.7	S57 20.0
02	298 26.3	217 37.4	55.6	128 13.0	02.9	141 45.4	55.4	125 56.6	38.4	Acrux	173 37.3	S62 59.7
03	313 28.8	232 41.3	55.0	143 14.4	02.3	156 47.5	55.3	140 58.9	38.3	Adhara	255 32.6	S28 56.8
04	328 31.3	247 45.3	54.3	158 15.7	01.8	171 49.6	55.2	156 01.3	38.3	Aldebaran	291 18.5	N16 28.1
05	343 33.7	262 49.3	53.7	173 17.0	01.2	186 51.7	55.0	171 03.6	38.2			
06	358 36.2	277 53.3	N20 53.1	188 18.3	N 5 00.7	201 53.9	N10 54.9	186 06.0	N 5 38.2	Alioth	166 42.6	N56 04.3
07	13 38.6	292 57.2	52.5	203 19.7	5 00.2	216 56.0	54.8	201 08.4	38.1	Alkaid	153 18.5	N49 25.0
08	28 41.1	308 01.2	51.8	218 21.0	4 59.6	231 58.1	54.6	216 10.7	38.1	Al Na'ir	28 15.0	S47 03.2
09	43 43.6	323 05.2	51.2	233 22.3	59.1	247 00.3	54.5	231 13.1	38.0	Alnilam	276 12.2	S 1 12.9
10	58 46.0	338 09.1	50.6	248 23.6	58.5	262 02.4	54.4	246 15.4	38.0	Alphard	218 21.0	S 8 34.5
11	73 48.5	353 13.1	50.0	263 24.9	58.0	277 04.5	54.2	261 17.8	37.9			
D 12	88 51.0	8 17.1	N20 49.4	278 26.3	N 4 57.5	292 06.7	N10 54.1	276 20.1	N 5 37.9	Alphecca	126 32.0	N26 47.0
A 13	103 53.4	23 21.0	48.7	293 27.6	56.9	307 08.8	54.0	291 22.5	37.8	Alpheratz	358 09.5	N28 58.7
Y 14	118 55.9	38 25.0	48.1	308 28.9	56.4	322 10.9	53.8	306 24.9	37.7	Altair	62 32.4	N 8 49.0
15	133 58.4	53 28.9	47.5	323 30.2	55.8	337 13.1	53.7	321 27.2	37.7	Ankaa	353 40.5	S42 24.6
16	149 00.8	68 32.9	46.9	338 31.6	55.3	352 15.2	53.5	336 29.6	37.6	Antares	112 56.7	S26 23.3
16	150 59.1	71 36.8	18.0	339 34.7	29.2	353 57.2	47.0	338 22.5	34.9	Suhail	11.2	S43 21.4
17	166 01.6	86 40.8	17.4	354 36.0	28.6	8 59.4	46.9	353 24.8	34.9			
18	181 04.0	101 44.1	N20 16.8	9 37.3	N 4 28.1	24 01.5	N10 46.8	8 27.2	N 5 34.8	Vega	80 55.5	N38 46.0
19	196 06.5	116 50.9	16.2	24 38.6	27.5	39 03.6	46.6	23 29.5	34.8	Zuben'ubi	137 33.0	S15 57.6
20	211 09.0	131 54.7	15.7	39 39.9	27.0	54 05.7	46.5	38 31.9	34.7		S.H.A.	Mer. Pass
21	226 11.4	146 58.5	15.1	54 41.2	26.4	69 07.8	46.3	53 34.2	34.7		° ′	h m
22	241 13.9	162 02.3	14.5	69 42.5	25.9	84 10.0	46.2	68 36.6	34.6	Venus	279 43.9	11 21
23	256 16.3	177 06.1	13.9	84 43.8	25.3	99 12.1	46.1	83 38.9	34.5	Mars	189 21.6	17 24
Mer. Pass.	h m 6 01.6	v 3.9	d 0.6	v 1.3	d 0.5	v 2.1	d 0.1	v 2.4	d 0.1	Jupiter Saturn	203 11.7 187 27.9	16 28 17 30

Suppose, for instance, that we need to know the GHA and Declination of Venus at 11:28:07 UT on 20 June:-

The left hand page of the Nautical Almanac's daily spread includes data for each planet in two columns, giving the GHA and Declination at hourly intervals – just as it does for the Sun. The only difference between Sun and Planet formats is that, there is an extra piece of information, called "v", at the bottom of the GHA column for each planet.

On June 20, for instance, Venus's v is 3′.9.

The reason for this is that Venus's GHA is not increasing at a constant fifteen degrees per hour. Between 10:00 and 11:00, for instance, it has increased from 338°09′.1 to 353°13′.1 – an increase of 15°04′.

PLANETS

CHAPTER 7

Armed with that information, finding the GHA at 10:28:07 is hardly advanced mathematics, but it is the kind of calculation that is tedious and prone to mistakes, so it's usually better to refer to the same table of **Increments and Corrections** as is used to help calculate the Sun's GHA and Declination.

[Table: Increments and Corrections for 28 and 29 minutes]

Looking at the left hand side of the 28-minute table, across the 7-second row, the figure in the "Sun Planets" column suggests that the GHA has increased by 7°01′.8. But this is based on the assumption that the GHA is increasing at a steady 15° per hour.

The v correction will put that right. Looking down the "v or d" column, we can see that 28 minutes' worth of 3′.9 adds up to 1′.9.

GHA Venus 11:00	353°13′.1 (v=+3.9)	Dec 11:00	N20°50′.0 (d=−0.6)
Increment for 28m07s	+ 7°01′.8	d corr'n for 28m	0′.3
	000°14′.9	Dec 11:28:07	N20°49′.7
v correction 28m07s	+ 1′.9		
GHA 11:28:07	000°16′.8		

The Planets always go round the same way, so the GHA correction is always added, but they don't always go round faster than the Sun, so it's important to make sure that you get the sign of the v correction right.

Astro Navigation Handbook

CHAPTER 7

Correcting the Sextant Altitude of a planet

Just like the Sun, the Sextant Altitude of a planet may need to be corrected for five errors.

Index error, dip, and refraction affect a planet sight in much the same way as a Sun sight:

Index error: found by checking the Sextant

Dip: found from the Altitude Correction Tables in the Nautical Almanac

Refraction: found in the Stars and Planets column of the Altitude Correction Tables in the Nautical Almanac.

The other two are different:

Semi-diameter: irrelevant for most planets, except Venus which is sometimes large enough to appear as a tiny disc – up to about a thirtieth of the diameter of the Sun – in a sextant telescope, and which appears to change shape in the same way (and for the same reason) as the Moon.

Parallax: an error of up to about $0'.2$, caused by the fact that the planets are not really on the surface of an infinitely large celestial sphere!

Combined corrections for the semi diameter, phases, and parallax of Venus, and for the parallax of Mars are included as a "monthly correction" in the Altitude Correction tables of the Nautical Almanac.

PLANETS

CHAPTER 7

ALTITUDE CORRECTION TABLES
10°–90°—SUN, STARS, PLANETS

Suppose, for instance, that Venus was shot as an evening star on May 30, with a Sextant Altitude of 17°23′.8. The sextant was 3.2 m above the waterline, and had an index error of 5′.3 on the arc:

Sextant Altitude	17°23′.8
Index error	− 5′.3
Observed Altitude	17°18′.5
Dip	− 3′.1
Apparent Altitude	17°15′.4
Refraction	− 3′.1
	17°12′.3
Monthly correction	+ 0′.6
True Altitude	17°12′.9

CHAPTER 7

Planning planet sights

The ancient Greeks called some stars "planetoi". The word means "wanderers", and of course it refers to what we now call "planets" – so called because they appear to wander slowly around the celestial sphere, sometimes fading, and sometimes disappearing altogether.

There is no point even thinking about taking a planet sight unless there is at least the possibility that it will be visible at the time.

So the first step in the process is to work out when you are likely to be taking your sights, using the procedure for finding sunrise, sunset, or twilight in Chapter 4 of this book.

There are several possible ways to find out which planets are likely to be visible at the time, but the most useful are probably the planet notes in the Nautical Almanac, or the Almanac's rather frightening-looking diagram showing how the time of meridian passage of each planet varies throughout the year. The point of the meridian passage diagram is that if a planet crosses your meridian at the same time as the Sun – at about local noon – then it will rise and set at about the same time as the Sun. So it will be effectively invisible, because it will only be above the horizon during daylight.

> If its meridian passage is slightly earlier – say between about 09:00 and 11:00 local time – it means that the planet is ahead of the Sun, so it will be visible above the eastern horizon before sunrise.

> If its meridian passage is a lot earlier – say between 00:00 and 02:00, it means that the planet is so far ahead of the Sun that it will be close to the western horizon and almost ready to set as the Sun rises.

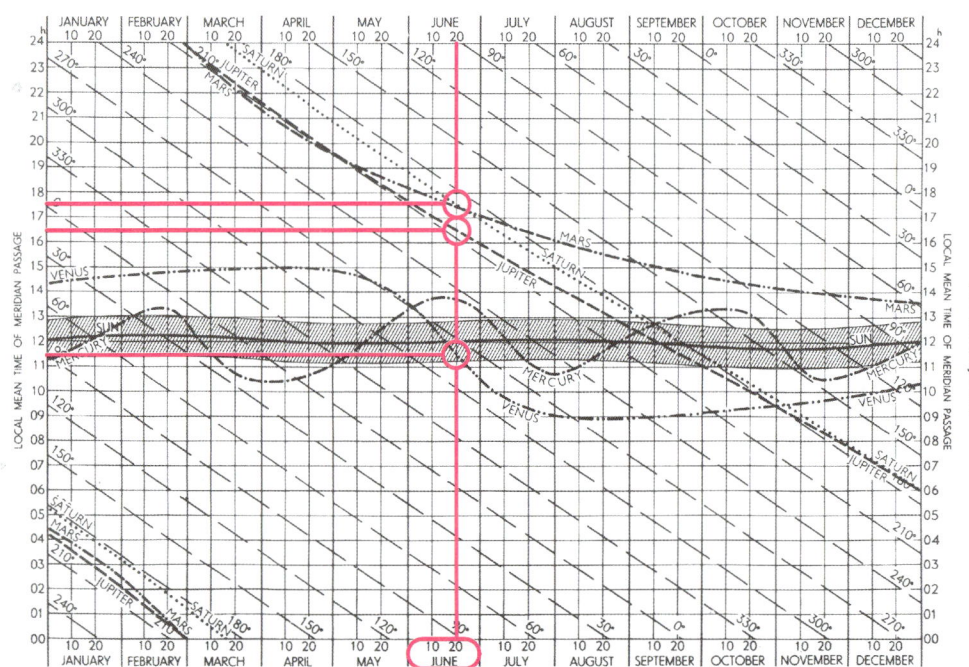

48   Astro Navigation Handbook

PLANETS

CHAPTER 7

The same logic applies if the planet's meridian passage is later than 12:00.

> If it is only two or three hours later – say between about 13:00 and 15:00 local time – it means that the planet is slightly behind the Sun, so it will be visible above the western horizon, after sunset.
>
> And if it is a lot later – say between 22:00 and 24:00 – then the planet is so far behind the Sun that it will have only just risen in the east when the Sun sets in the west.

Suppose, for instance, that we are on passage from the English Channel to the Med, on 20 June, and that our estimated position at 1800UT is 45°38'.8N 8°30'W. What time is civil twilight? And what planets will be visible?

Time of Twilight from Almanac	20 31
Longitude correction (8°30'W)	+00 34
Time of Twilight at 45°30'N 8°30'W (UT)	21 05

Looking at the Meridian Passage diagram for 20 June:
Venus *Mer.Pass is at about 11:30, so it is very close to the Sun: if it is visible at all, it will be as a "morning star".*
Mars *and* **Saturn** *are both crossing the Meridian at about 17:30. They should both be visible, fairly high in the sky, but they are likely to be so close together that there is a risk of confusing the two.*
Jupiter's *Mer.Pass is at about 16:30.*

Having decided that Jupiter is probably the one to go for, we could then help ourselves to make a positive identification of it by doing a very rough calculation, using the data given in the Nautical Almanac and the Sight Reduction Tables. There's no need for precision, at this stage:

GHA Jupiter @ 21:00	67°	Dec Jupiter @ 21:00	N11°
Chos. Pos.	46°N 8°		
LHA	59°		

From the Sight Reduction Tables: $H_c = 29°$, $Z = 105°$ so $Z_n = 255°$

Astro Navigation Handbook

CHAPTER 7

The whole calculation

Suppose that we are on passage from the English Channel to the Med, on 20 June, and that our last fix was the Merpass-run-Sun at 1828, at 45°38'.8N 8°31'.4W. At about 20:35 UT, after following a ground track of 185° for 15 miles, a series of sights are taken of Jupiter: the average time is 20:35:42 UT and the average sextant altitude is 33°37'.7. The sextant is 3.2 m above the waterline, and its index error is 5'.3 on the arc:

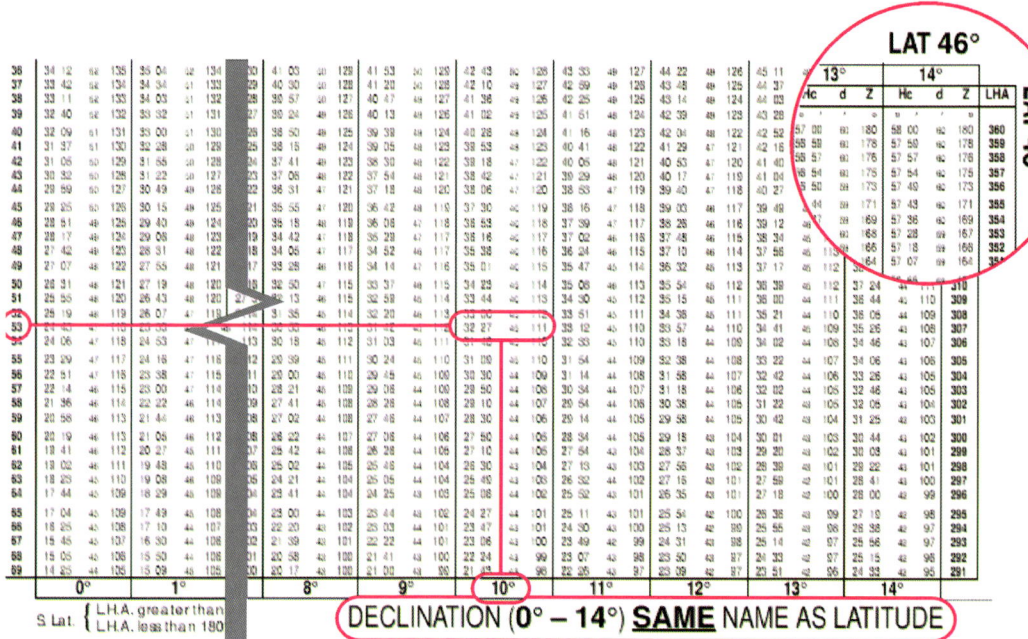

Sextant Altitude	33°37'.7		from sextant reading
Index error	− 5'.3		from sextant adjustment
Observed Altitude	33°32'.4		
Dip	− 3'.1		from Almanac Altitude Correction Tables
Apparent Altitude	33°29'.3		
Refraction	− 1'.5		from Almanac Altitude Correction Tables
H_o	33°27'.8		
GHA at 20:00	52° 23'.7 (v = +2.1)		from Almanac Daily Page
inc. for 35m 42s	+8° 55'.5		from Almanac Increments and Corrections
	61° 19'.2		
v corr'n	+ 1'.2		from Almanac Increments and Corrections
GHA at 20:35:42	61° 20'.4		
Dec at 20:00	N 10°53'.0 (d = −0.1)		from Almanac Daily Page
inc. for 35m 42s	− 0'.1		from Almanac Increments and Corrections
Dec at 20:35:42	N 10°52'.9		

50 **Astro Navigation Handbook**

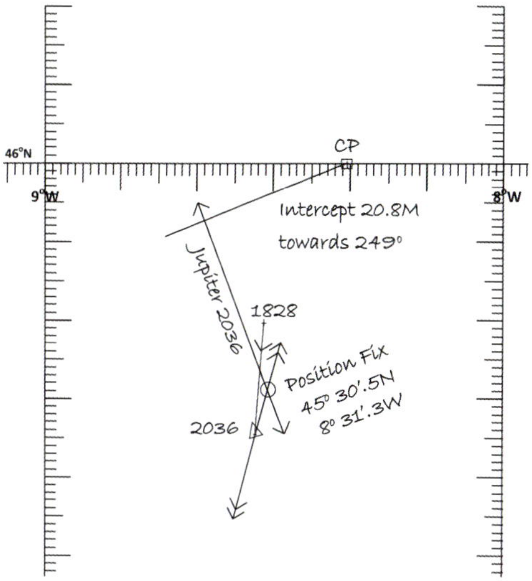

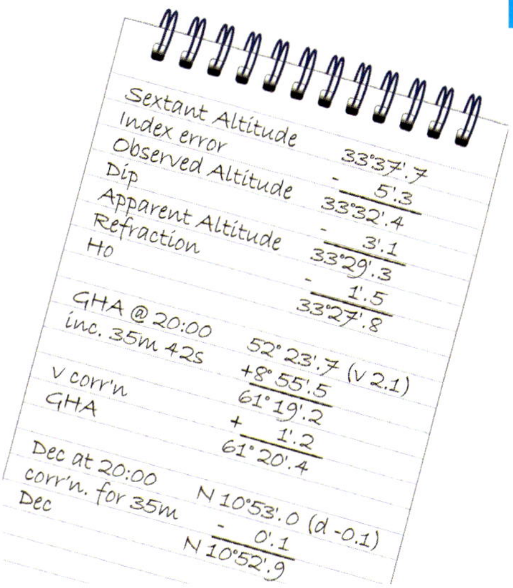

PLANETS

CHAPTER 7

Sextant Altitude   33°37'.7
Index error   −   5'.3
Observed Altitude   33°32'.4
Dip   −   3'.1
Apparent Altitude   33°29'.3
Refraction   −   1'.5
Ho   33°27'.8

GHA @ 20:00
inc. 35m 42s   52° 23'.7
                         +8° 55'.5   (V 2.1)
v corr'n   61° 19'.2
GHA   +   1'.2
                          61° 20'.4

Dec at 20:00   N 10°53'.0 (d −0.1)
corr'n. for 35m   −   0'.1
Dec   N 10°52'.9

GHA at 20:35:42	61° 20'.4	from earlier calculation
Chosen Position 46°N	8° 20'.4W	to make LHA a whole number
LHA	53°	
H_c	32°27' (d = +45) Z = 111	from Sight Reduction Tables
Corr'n for minutes of Dec	40'	from Sight Reduction Tables
H_c	33°07' Zn = 249°	
H_c	33°07'	from previous calculation
H_o	33°27'.8	from earlier calculation
Intercept	20'.8 Towards 249°	

Notice that in this case, H_c (the "tabulated" altitude) is smaller than H_o (the true altitude). This means that the position line must be closer to the body than the chosen position, so the intercept has to be drawn and measured towards the azimuth.

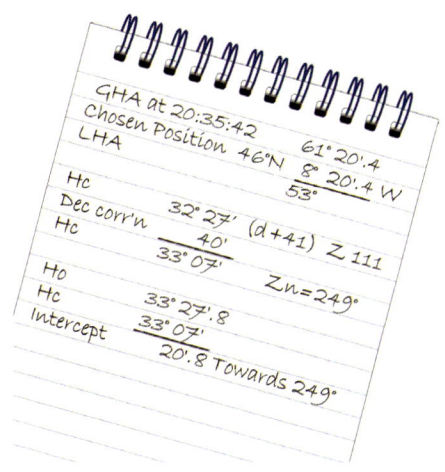

Astro Navigation Handbook | 51

Chapter 8: Morning And Evening Stars

Morning and evening stars have been the bane of the lives of generations of merchant navy cadets and Royal Navy midships. Technically, they weren't very different from sun or planet sights. They still involved correcting the sextant altitude, working out the LHA and declination, and using sight reduction tables to work out calculated altitudes to compare with the corrected sextant altitudes.

But there were more of them – usually four or five at a time. That, of course, is the great virtue of star sights: the fact that there are dozens of stars available within minutes of sunset or sunrise means that you can get several position lines more or less simultaneously, intersecting with each other to produce a complete fix. But from the point of view of a cadet or midship, it also means that there are four or five times as many opportunities to make a mistake, and that the whole process takes four or five times as long – just when you're ready for either breakfast or bed!

But then someone told us about Volume 1 of the Air Sight Reduction Tables – usually known as "Seven Selected Stars".

The principle of star sights

In principle, a star sight is almost exactly the same as a planet sight. The main difference is in the way the Nautical Almanac presents the GHA and Declination of the stars.

If the data for each of the fifty seven "navigational stars" were presented individually, as it is for the four planets, the Almanac would need at least an extra thousand pages.

But the stars – unlike the planets – do not "wander". They seem to be fixed to the inner surface of the celestial sphere, so although the whole universe appears to spin around the Earth, the stars stay in almost exactly the same positions, relative to each other, for years on end.

So instead of having to give the GHA and declination of every star at hourly intervals throughout the year, the Nautical Almanac can save paper by using just two angles.

The following extract from the Almanac for instance, gives the position of Arcturus as 146°18′.5 N 19°17′.2.

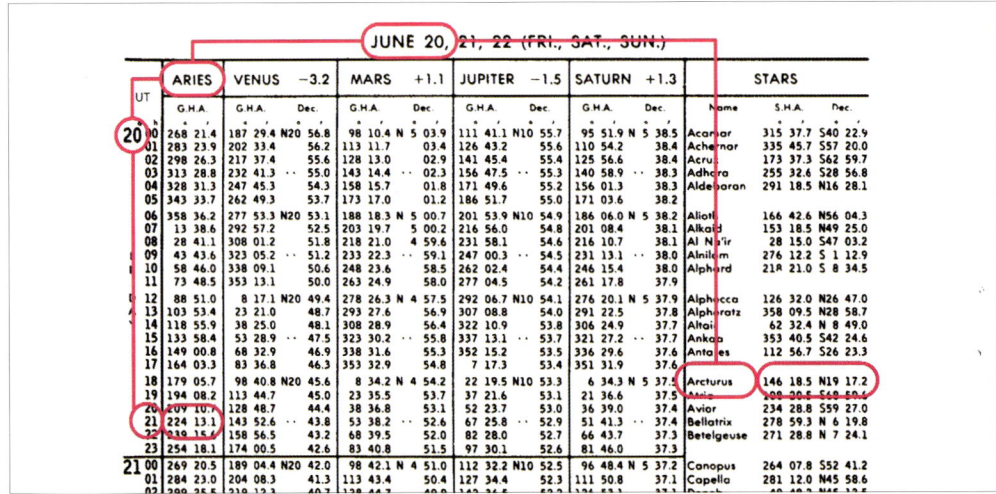

MORNING AND EVENING STARS

CHAPTER 8

The second of the two angles is its Declination: just as for the Sun and planets, it's a measure of how far the star is from the celestial Equator.

The first angle is called the Sidereal Hour Angle, and it's a measure of how far west the star lies, compared with an invisible reference point called the First Point of Aries.

The First Point of Aries

It takes the Earth a year to make one complete orbit of the Sun.

In the Earth-centred representation of the universe that we use for astro navigation, the effect is that every year, the Sun travels right round the celestial sphere, following a path called the Ecliptic.

In the northern summer, the Sun is just over 23 degrees north of the celestial equator, whilst in the northern winter it is just over 23 degrees south of the Equator. Only twice a year – on about the 20th of March and the 22nd of September – is the sun directly on the celestial equator. The Ecliptic, in other words, is tilted, intersecting with the Equator at just two points.

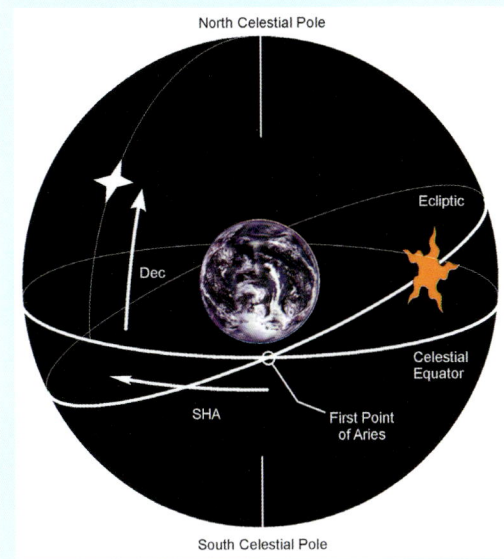

One of these two – the point at which the sun crosses the Equator into the northern hemisphere – is the First Point of Aries.

To find the star's Greenwich Hour Angle, we need to add the GHA of the first point of Aries to the Sidereal Hour Angle of the star:

Suppose, for instance, that at 21:28:06UT on 20 June, at approximately 45°22'N 8°23'W, we've measured the altitude of a star high in the south south west that is probably Arcturus. The Sextant Altitude is 62°56'.3, with an Index error of 5'.3 on the arc and a height of eye of 3.2 metres.

The Almanac's daily page gives the GHA of the First Point of Aries (abbreviated to "Aries") as 224°13'.1 at 21:00, and the Increments and Corrections table shows that the correction for the odd minutes and seconds is 7°02'.7.

Astro Navigation Handbook | 53

Chapter 8

It's worth noticing that the corrections for "Aries" are not quite the same as those for the Sun and planets. Using the wrong column won't make a complete nonsense of your fix, but it could easily build in an unnecessary error of a mile or two.

So the GHA of Aries is:

GHA Aries at 21:00UT	224°13'.1	from Almanac Daily Page
Correction for 28m 06s	7°02'.7	from Almanac Increments and Corrections
GHA Aries at 21:28:06	231°15'.8	

To this, we now add the SHA of the star to find its GHA:

GHA Aries at 21:28:06	231°15'.8	from earlier calculation
SHA Arcturus	146°18'.5	from Almanac Daily Page
GHA Arcturus at 21:28:06	377°34'.3	
	360°00'.0	to make GHA less than 360°
GHA Arcturus at 21:28:06	17°34'.3	

And finally, because the sight reduction tables need the local hour angle (LHA), we need to add or subtract our chosen longitude:

GHA Arcturus at 21:28:06	17°34'.3	from earlier calculation
Chosen Position 45°N	- 8°34'.3 W	to make LHA a whole number
LHA Arcturus	9°	
Declination Arcturus	N19°17'.2	from Almanac Daily Page

From here on, having found the Local Hour Angle and knowing the Declination, the calculation is exactly the same as it would be for a planet: the Sextant Altitude has to be corrected for Index error, Dip, and refraction, to obtain the True Altitude (H_o), which can then be compared with the Calculated Altitude (H_c) from the Sight Reduction Tables to obtain the Intercept and Azimuth.

Sextant Altitude	62°56'.3	from sextant reading
Index error	- 5'.3	from sextant adjustment
Observed Altitude	62°51'.0	
Dip	- 3'.1	from Almanac Altitude Correction Tables
Apparent Altitude	62°47'.9	
Refraction	- 0'.5	from Almanac Altitude Correction Tables
H_o	62°47'.4	
H_c	62°57'	(d = +58) Z = 161 from Sight Reduction Tables
Corr'n for minutes of Dec	16'	from Sight Reduction Tables
H_c	63°13'	Zn = 199°
H_c	63°13'	from previous calculation
H_o	62°47'.4	from earlier calculation
Intercept	25'.6	Away 199°

Astro Navigation Handbook

MORNING AND EVENING STARS

CHAPTER 8

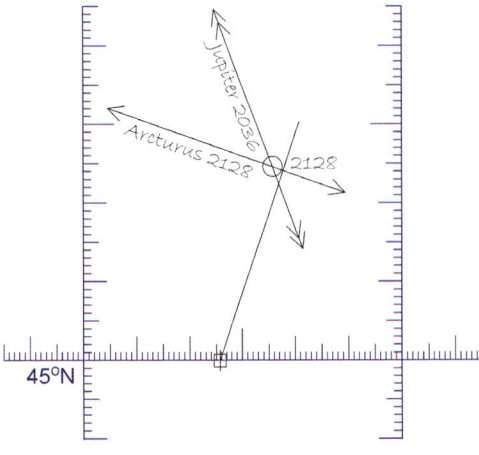

In this case, the Calculated Altitude (H_c) is larger than the True Altitude (H_o) so the chosen position must be closer to the star than the true position, so the intercept must be drawn and measured away from the Azimuth. (see illustration)

So what's wrong with the old way?

The only real problem in using this method to work out a star sight is that the Air Sight Reduction Tables can only handle declinations of less than 30° – which rules out roughly half of the navigational stars, including some of the very brightest and most useful.

This isn't a problem for anyone using Marine Sight Reduction Tables – but they are so much bigger, heavier, more expensive and less user-friendly than the Air Sight Tables that relatively few navigators – particularly on small craft – still use them.

Preparing for star sights

In order to take a star sight, you need to be able to see the horizon clearly, as well as the star. This means that the "window of opportunity" is very much the same as for a planet sight. If anything, it's a slightly smaller window, because stars are generally less bright than planets, so they appear later in the evening and disappear earlier in the morning.

So the first step in any planning process is to work out the time of civil and nautical twilight, just as when planning a planet sight.

Then, it is worth planning which stars you are likely to "shoot", and working out where you expect to see each one. This doesn't prevent you from taking an opportunist shot at any bright star you happen to see, but it is particularly useful in the evening, because if you know where to look, you stand a much better chance of seeing the stars you want while the horizon is still clear than if you just stand on deck gawping up into the darkening sky!

Astro Navigation Handbook | 55

CHAPTER 8

Identifying stars

For centuries, sailors and stargazers have used the constellations – and the somewhat fanciful names given to them by ancient astronomers – as ways to identify particular stars.

Rigel, for instance, is Orion's left knee; Betelgeuse is his right shoulder; and you can find Arcturus by extending the handle of the Plough.

But this doesn't work if you can't see the constellations because the sky is too light or there's too much cloud. So although it might be useful for a fix in the early morning, when you can watch the constellations fade as dawn breaks, it's not much use for evening stars. By the time you can see the constellations, you probably won't be able to see the horizon.

There are several alternatives, of which two are particularly useful.

Precomputed sights

Some navigators go to the extent of working out the entire sight beforehand, so that they can set the sextant to the expected altitude for each star in advance. Stars are often visible through the sextant telescope when it is still too light for them to be seen with the naked eye.

This is a particularly useful technique if you use a programmable calculator or computer to work out the sight, because the calculator doesn't mind doing a lot of number crunching. But doing the whole job with a pencil and paper can be time consuming.

Planisphere or Starfinder

A planisphere consists of a star map, printed on a circular plastic base, and a rotating mask that restricts your view of the star map to an oval window, showing just the stars that are visible at a particular date and time.

MORNING AND EVENING STARS

CHAPTER 8

To use it, you rotate the upper layer until the local time of twilight (on the upper layer) is against the date (on the base). The oval window then represents the sky as you would see it if you were lying on your back and looking straight upwards.

Simple planispheres suffer a couple of drawbacks.

One is that each planisphere is technically correct for only one latitude. It will serve its purpose within about five degrees of its designated latitude, but becomes progressively less accurate until at about ten degrees or so from its designated latitude, it becomes almost useless. To overcome this, manufacturers make several different editions of each planisphere, each valid for a different latitude.

The other is that representing half of the celestial sphere on a flat map inevitably introduces huge distortions. That is why the window of the planisphere has to be oval, rather than circular. But it can make it difficult to get any more than a rough idea of the layout of the sky.

A more sophisticated alternative is Weems and Plath Starfinder 2102-D, which consists of a circular star chart and a pack of removable templates. To set it up, you pick the template that most nearly matches your latitude, and rotate it until the arrow printed on it matches the Local Hour Angle of Aries printed around the edge of the base. The template has a grid of Altitude and Azimuth printed on it, allowing the position of each star to be found quite accurately.

Seven Selected Stars

A book known as "Air Sight Reduction Tables Volume 1", or more often as "Seven Selected Stars", is the answer to a midship's prayer, simplifying the planning and identification, and cutting out most of the arithmetic involved in a series of star sights.

It works on the basis that for any given combination of Latitude and Local Hour Angle of Aries, the Altitude and Azimuth of each star can be calculated – and will stay effectively the same for several years. Not only that, but for any given combination of Latitude and LHA, most navigators are likely to choose the same stars.

It can't do anything to simplify the correction of Sextant Altitude to True Altitude, nor to help find the Local Hour Angle of Aries: those two bits of the job are exactly the same as for the longer calculation.

But once you have found the page corresponding to your latitude and the line corresponding to the Local Hour Angle of Aries, the Altitude and Azimuth of each of seven selected stars can be read off straight from the tables. It requires no further correction or interpolation.

CHAPTER 8

LHA	Hc Zn	Hc Zn	Hc Zn	Hc Zn	Hc Zn	Hc Zn	Hc Zn
	♦Mirfak	Alpheratz	♦ALTAIR	Rasalhague	♦ARCTURUS	Alkaid	Kochab
270	15 18 025	20 41 069	42 56 142	52 12 148	36 07 258	50 19 294	58 50 337
271	15 34 026	21 17 070	43 19 143	52 04 192	35 30 257	49 44 295	58 35 337
272	15 51 026	21 53 071	43 42 144	51 56 194	34 5 258	49 09 295	58 20 337
273	16 08 027	22 30 071	44 05 145	51 49 195	34 19 259	48 34 296	58 05 337
274	16 26 027	23 06 072	44 28 147	51 39 197	33 36 260	48 00 296	57 49 337
275	16 44 028	23 43 073	44 49 148	51 28 198	32 58 261	47 25 297	57 34 336
276	17 02 029	24 20 073	45 09 149	51 17 200	32 20 262	46 51 297	57 18 336
277	17 21 029	24 57 074	45 28 151	50 53 201	31 42 262	46 16 298	57 03 336
278	17 40 030	25 34 075	45 45 152	50 41 203	31 04 263	45 42 298	56 47 336
279	17 59 030	26 11 075	46 01 153	50 28 204	30 26 264	45 08 299	56 31 336
280	18 19 031	26 48 076	46 20 155	50 13 206	29 47 265	44 34 299	56 15 336
281	18 39 032	27 26 077	46 34 156	47 55 207	29 09 266	44 01 299	56 00 336
282	19 00 032	28 03 077	46 51 157	49 37 209	28 30 266	43 27 300	55 44 335
283	19 20 033	28 41 078	47 06 159	49 18 210	27 52 267	42 54 300	55 28 335
284	19 41 033	29 19 079	47 19 160	48 58 211	27 13 268	42 21 301	55 11 335
	♦Mirfak	Alpheratz	♦ALTAIR	Rasalhague	♦ARCTURUS	Alkaid	Kochab
285	20 03 034	29 57 079	47 32 162	48 38 213	26 35 269	41 48 301	54 55 335
286	20 24 034	30 35 080	47 44 163	48 17 214	25 56 270	41 15 302	54 39 335
287	20 46 035	31 13 081	47 54 164	47 55 215	25 17 270	40 42 302	54 23 335
288	21 09 036	31 51 082	48 04 166	47 32 217	24 39 271	40 10 303	54 07 335
289	21 31 036	32 29 082	48 13 167	47 08 218	24 00 272	39 37 303	53 50 335
290	21 54 037	33 07 083	48 21 169	46 44 219	23 22 273	39 05 304	53 34 335
291	22 17 037	33 46 084	48 28 170	46 19 221	22 43 273	38 33 304	53 18 335
292	22 41 038	34 24 084	48 34 172	45 54 222	22 05 274	38 01 305	53 02 335
293	23 05 038	35 02 085	48 39 173	45 28 223	21 26 275	37 30 305	52 45 335
294	23 29 039	35 41 086	48 43 175	45 01 224	20 48 276	36 58 306	52 29 335
295	23 53 040	36 19 087	48 46 176	44 34 226	20 10 276	36 27 306	52 13 335
296	24 18 040	36 58 087	48 48 178	44 06 227	19 31 277	35 56 307	51 56 335
297	24 43 041	37 36 088	48 49 179	43 37 228	18 53 278	35 25 307	51 40 335
298	25 08 041	38 15 089	48 49 181	43 08 229	18 15 279	34 54 308	51 24 335
299	25 34 042	38 54 090	48 48 182	42 39 230	17 37 279	34 24 308	51 08 335
	CAPELLA	♦Alpheratz	Enif	ALTAIR	♦Rasalhague	Alphecca	♦Kochab
300	12 24 028	39 32 090	44 28 143	48 46 184	42 09 232	35 00 271	50 51 335
301	12 42 029	40 11 091	44 51 144	48 43 185	41 39 233	34 22 272	50 35 335
302	13 01 029	40 49 092	45 13 146	48 38 187	41 08 234	33 43 273	50 19 335
303	13 20 030	41 28 093	45 34 147	48 33 188	40 36 235	33 05 273	50 03 335
304	13 39 030	42 06 093	45 55 148	48 27 190	40 05 236	32 26 274	49 47 335
305	13 59 031	42 45 094	46 15 150	48 20 191	39 33 237	31 48 275	49 31 336
306	14 19 032	43 23 095	46 34 151	48 12 193	39 00 238	31 09 276	49 15 336
307	14 40 032	44 02 096	46 52 152	48 03 194	38 27 239	30 31 276	48 59 336
308	15 01 033	44 40 097	47 10 154	47 53 196	37 54 240	29 53 277	48 43 336
309	15 22 034	45 18 098	47 26 155	47 42 197	37 20 241	29 14 278	48 27 336
310	15 43 034	45 56 098	47 42 157	47 31 199	36 46 242	28 36 279	48 12 336
311	16 05 035	46 34 099	47 57 158	47 18 200	36 12 243	27 58 279	47 56 336
312	16 27 035	47 12 100	48 11 159	47 04 201	35 38 244	27 20 280	47 40 336
313	16 50 036	47 50 101	48 24 161	46 50 203	35 03 245	26 42 281	47 25 336
314	17 13 037	48 28 102	48 37 162	46 34 204	34 28 246	26 04 281	47 10 336

LAT 50°N

As the name suggests, Seven Selected Stars does not give details of every possible star, so it is important to make sure that you use it at the planning stage, to make sure the stars you shoot are the ones for which it gives answers! So the first stage is to plan the shoot:

On 21 September, at approximately 49°40'N 42°35'W, it is intended to take sights of evening stars.

	Civil Twilight	Nautical Twilight
Time of Twilight from Almanac 50°	1830	1908
Longitude correction (42°30'W)	+0250	+0250
Time of Twilight at 50°00'N 42°30'W (UT)	2120	2158
GHA Aries at 2100	315°53'.0	315°53'.0
Correction for minutes	5°06'.8	14°32'.4
GHA Aries at Twilight	320°59'.8	330°25'.4
Chosen Position 50°N	42°59'.8	42°25'.4
LHA Aries	278°	288°

Looking at the page headed 50°N in Seven Selected Stars, we can see that while the LHA is between 278° and 288°, the seven selected stars are Mirfak, Alpheratz, Altair, Rasalhague, Arcturus, Alkaid and Kochab.

58 Astro Navigation Handbook

MORNING AND EVENING STARS

CHAPTER 8

Altair and Arcturus are in capitals, because they are particularly bright stars.

Mirfak, Altair and Arcturus are marked with a diamond symbol to show that they are particularly recommended as the best combination of stars to make a fix: they are at reasonable altitudes – neither too high or too low – and they are well spread to give a good angle of cut between the position lines.

On 21 September, at approximately 49° 40′N 42° 35′, sights are taken of evening stars. Index error was 5′.3 on the arc and the height of eye was 3.2 metres. The averaged times and sextant altitudes were:

Altair	21 28 14	46°54′.4
Arcturus	21 31 04	29°11′.8
Rasalhague	21 35 21	49°58′.4

		Altair	**Arcturus**	**Rasalhague**
GHA Aries at 2100		315°53′.0	315°53′.0	315°53′.0
Correction for min/secs		7°04′.7	7°47′.3	8°51′.7
GHA Aries at sight		322°57′.7	323°40′.3	324°44′.7
Chosen Position	50°N	42°57′.7	42°40′.3	42°44′.7
LHA Aries		280°	281°	282°
Sextant Altitude		46°54′.4	29°11′.8	49°58′.4
Index error		- 5′.3	- 5′.3	- 5′.3
Observed Altitude		46°49′.1	29°06′.5	49°53′.1
Dip		- 3′.1	- 3′.1	- 3′.1
Apparent Altitude		46°46′.0	29°03′.4	49°50′.0
Refraction		- 0′.9	- 1′.7	- 0′.8
H_o		46°45′.1	29°01′.7	49°49′.2
H_c (from Seven Sel. Stars)		46°20′	29°09′	49°37′
Intercept		25′.1	7′.3	12′.2
Z_n (from Seven Sel. Stars)		155° To	266° Away	209° To

Plotting the position line from each calculation is exactly the same as if it has been derived from the sun or a planet: the main difference is that there are more of them.

Astro Navigation Handbook

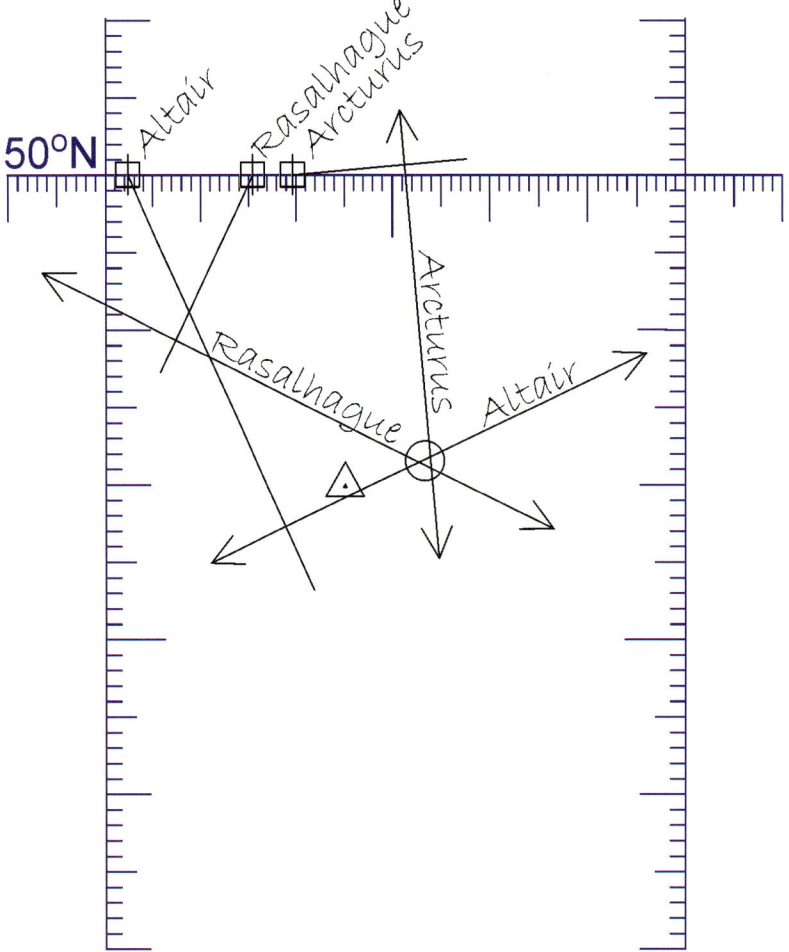

Navigators of fast boats, or who take a long time over their sights need to be aware of the fact that although evening stars are sometimes called "simultaneous sights", they aren't really simultaneous.

In this example, there was a seven minute gap between the first and the last. At sailing yacht or displacement motor cruiser speeds, this is probably less than a mile, so it is hardly worth worrying about. At twenty knots, however, we'd have moved nearly two and a half miles. Strictly speaking, then, we should treat this as a running fix, moving the two first position lines onwards to correspond with the boat's movement while the fix was being taken.

Chapter 9: Polaris

Polaris is probably the one star that most people could name – even if they couldn't actually point to it! But there's nothing particularly special about it, other than that its Declination of N89° 18' means that it is less than one degree from the celestial North Pole.

If it were exactly on the North Pole, its True Altitude would correspond with the observer's latitude.

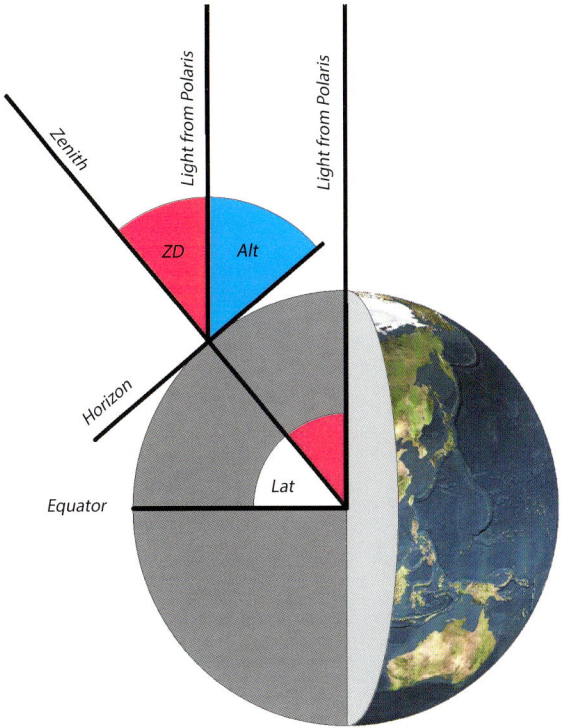

The fact that it is nearly-but-not-quite on the pole means that we can still use this principle, but with a few small corrections.

Those corrections are given in the **Polaris Tables** in the Nautical Almanac, and are applied by using the formula:

Latitude = True Altitude + a_0 + a_1 + a_2 - 1°

Astro Navigation Handbook

CHAPTER 9

POLARIS (POLE STAR) TABLES, 1980
FOR DETERMINING LATITUDE FROM SEXTANT ALTITUDE AND FOR AZIMUTH

L.H.A. ARIES	120°–129°	130°–139°	140°–149°	150°–159°	160°–169°	170°–179°	180°–189°	190°–199°	200°–209°	210°–219°	220°–229°	230°–239°
	a_0	a_0	a_0	a_0	a_0	a_0	a_0	a_0	a_0	a_0	a_0	a_0
0	0 56·5	1 05·1	1 13·6	1 21·5	1 28·8	1 35·1	1 40·4	1 44·4	1 47·0	1 48·2	1 48·0	1 46·2
1	57·4	06·0	14·4	22·3	29·4	35·7	40·8	44·7	47·2	48·3	47·8	46·0
2	58·2	06·8	15·2	23·0	30·1	36·3	41·3	45·0	47·4	48·3	47·7	45·7
3	0 59·1	07·7	16·0	23·8	30·8	36·8	41·7	45·3	47·5	48·3	47·6	45·4
4	1 00·0	08·5	16·8	24·5	31·4	37·4	42·1	45·6	47·7	48·3	47·4	45·1
5	1 00·8	1 09·4	1 17·6	1 25·2	1 32·1	1 37·9	1 42·5	1 45·9	1 47·8	1 48·3	1 47·3	1 44·8
6	01·7	10·2	18·4	26·0	32·7	38·4	42·9	46·1	47·9	48·2	47·1	44·5
7	02·6	11·1	19·2	26·7	33·3	38·9	43·3	46·4	48·0	48·2	46·9	44·1
8	03·4	11·9	20·0	27·4	33·9	39·4	43·7	46·6	48·1	48·1	46·7	43·8
9	04·3	12·7	20·7	28·1	34·5	39·9	44·0	46·8	48·2	48·0	46·4	43·4
10	1 05·1	1 13·6	1 21·5	1 28·8	1 35·1	1 40·4	1 44·4	1 47·0	1 48·2	1 48·0	1 46·2	1 43·0

Lat.	a_1	a_1	a_1	a_1	a_1	a_1	a_1	a_1	a_1	a_1	a_1	a_1
0	0·2	0·2	0·2	0·3	0·4	0·4	0·5	0·6	0·6	0·6	0·6	0·5
10	·2	·3	·3	·3	·4	·5	·5	·6	·6	·6	·6	·5
20	·3	·3	·3	·4	·4	·5	·5	·6	·6	·6	·6	·6
30	·4	·4	·4	·4	·5	·5	·6	·6	·6	·6	·6	·6
40	0·5	0·5	0·5	0·5	0·5	0·6	0·6	0·6	0·6	0·6	0·6	0·6
45	·5	·5	·5	·6	·6	·6	·6	·6	·6	·6	·6	·6
50	·6	·6	·6	·6	·6	·6	·6	·6	·6	·6	·6	·6
55	·7	·7	·7	·7	·6	·6	·6	·6	·6	·6	·6	·6
60	·8	·8	·8	·7	·7	·7	·6	·6	·6	·6	·6	·6
62	0·8	0·8	0·8	0·8	0·7	0·7	0·7	0·6	0·6	0·6	0·6	0·6
64	0·9	0·9	·9	·8	·8	·7	·7	·6	·6	·6	·6	·6
66	1·0	1·0	0·9	·9	·8	·7	·7	·6	·6	·6	·6	·7
68	1·1	1·0	1·0	0·9	0·9	0·8	0·7	0·6	0·6	0·6	0·6	0·7

Month	a_2	a_2	a_2	a_2	a_2	a_2	a_2	a_2	a_2	a_2	a_2	a_2
Jan.	0·6	0·6	0·6	0·5	0·5	0·5	0·5	0·5	0·5	0·5	0·5	0·5
Feb.	·8	·7	·7	·7	·6	·6	·6	·5	·5	·5	·5	·4
Mar.	0·9	0·9	0·9	0·8	·8	·8	·7	·7	·6	·6	·5	·5
Apr.	1·0	1·0	1·0	1·0	0·9	0·9	0·9	0·8	0·8	0·7	0·6	0·6
May	0·9	1·0	1·0	1·0	1·0	1·0	1·0	0·9	0·9	0·8	·8	·7
June	·8	0·9	0·9	1·0	1·0	1·0	1·0	1·0	1·0	1·0	0·9	·9
July	0·7	0·7	0·8	0·8	0·9	0·9	1·0	1·0	1·0	1·0	1·0	0·9
Aug.	·5	·6	·6	·7	·7	·8	0·8	0·9	0·9	0·9	1·0	1·0
Sept.	·4	·4	·4	·5	·6	·6	·7	·7	·8	·8	0·9	0·9
Oct.	0·3	0·3	0·3	0·3	0·4	0·4	0·5	0·5	0·6	0·7	0·7	0·8
Nov.	·2	·2	·2	·2	·2	·3	·3	·4	·4	·5	·5	·6
Dec.	0·3	0·3	0·2	0·2	0·2	0·2	0·2	0·2	0·3	0·3	0·4	0·4

Lat.					AZIMUTH							
0	359·2	359·2	359·2	359·3	359·4	359·5	359·6	359·7	359·9	0·0	0·2	0·3
20	359·1	359·1	359·2	359·3	359·3	359·5	359·6	359·7	359·9	0·0	0·2	0·3
40	358·9	358·9	359·0	359·1	359·2	359·3	359·5	359·7	359·8	0·0	0·2	0·4
50	358·7	358·7	358·8	358·9	359·1	359·2	359·4	359·6	359·8	0·0	0·3	0·5
55	358·6	358·6	358·7	358·8	358·9	359·1	359·3	359·6	359·8	0·0	0·3	0·5
60	358·4	358·4	358·5	358·6	358·8	359·0	359·2	359·5	359·8	0·1	0·3	0·6
65	358·1	358·1	358·2	358·4	358·6	358·8	359·1	359·4	359·7	0·1	0·4	0·7

ILLUSTRATION

On 1980 April 21 at UT.
23ʰ 18ᵐ 56ˢ in longitude
W. 37° 14′ the apparent altitude (corrected for refraction), H_o, of Polaris was 49° 31′·6.

From the daily pages:
G.H.A. Aries (23ʰ)   195° 09′·8
Increment (18ᵐ 56ˢ)   4 44·8
Longitude (west)   −37 14
L.H.A. Aries   162 41

H_o 49° 31′·6
a_0 (argument 162° 41′)   1 30·6
a_1 (lat. 50° approx.)   0·6
a_2 (April)   0·9
                                    ─────────
Sum −1° = Lat. =   50 03·7

POLARIS

CHAPTER 9

In practice, the procedure is:-
1. Find the Local Hour Angle of Aries – an accuracy of one degree is sufficient.
2. Correct the Sextant Altitude to the True Altitude in the usual way, by allowing for index error, refraction and dip.
3. Find the appropriate column of the Polaris Table, according to the LHA of Aries.
4. Use the final digit of the LHA of Aries to find the appropriate row in the top section of the table, to pick out the value of a_0.
5. In the same column of the table, use your approximate latitude to find the appropriate row of the middle section of the table, to pick out the value of a_1.
6. In the same column of the table, use the month of the year to find the appropriate row of the bottom section of the table, to pick out the value of a_2.
7. Add a_0, a_1, and a_2 to the True Altitude, and subtract 1°.
8. The answer is your latitude.

On 20 June, at approximately 45°22′N 8°23′W, a sight of Polaris was taken as one of the evening stars. Index error was 5′.3 on the arc and the height of eye was 3.2 metres. The averaged time was 21:34UT and the averaged sextant altitude was 44° 43′.8.

GHA Aries at 21:00UT	224°13′.1
Correction for 34m	8°31′.4
GHA Aries at 21:34	232°44′.5
Longitude	8°23′.0
LHA Aries	224°21′.5
Sextant Altitude	44°43′.8
Index error	- 5′.3
Observed Altitude	44°38′.5
Dip	- 3′.1
Apparent Altitude	44°35′.4
Refraction	- 1′.0
H_o	44°34′.4
a_0	1°47′.4
a_1	0′.6
a_2	0′.9
	46°23′.3
-1	- 1°00′.0
Latitude	45°23′.3 N

Astro Navigation Handbook

Chapter 10: The Moon

Everyone knows the Moon. It's our nearest neighbour in space, so close that it appears to be the same size as the Sun, and it's the second brightest body in the sky – so bright that it is often visible in daylight. And yet it is probably the last choice object for astro navigation.

There are several reasons for this, partly offset by one important advantage:

The drawbacks are:-
- It moves around the celestial sphere much faster than any other heavenly body, making precise timing critical.
- It is so close that parallax is significant.
- It is so close that it appears to vary in size, depending where it is in its orbit and where it is in relation to the observer's zenith.
- It is seldom bright enough to illuminate the whole horizon, but it appears to distort the visible horizon, often making it seem lower than it really is.
- Its crescent shape means that you may have to measure the altitude of the upper limb (upper edge), rather than the lower limb, as one usually does when dealing with the sun. Whilst this is hardly a big issue, it's yet another opportunity for mistakes.

The advantage is that at certain times of each month the moon provides an easily visible and identifiable source of a position line that can be crossed with a position line from the Sun.

THE MOON

CHAPTER 10

Finding the Greenwich Hour Angle and Declination of the Moon

The procedure for finding the GHA and Declination of the Moon is almost exactly the same as for a planet. The only difference – apart from the need for greater precision in time keeping and greater accuracy, which mean that the v and d corrections are given for every hour – is that the almanac supplies an extra column of data, labelled "H.P.", for "Horizontal Parallax".

JUNE 20, 21, 22 (FRI., SAT., SUN.)

UT	SUN G.H.A.	SUN Dec.	MOON G.H.A.	MOON v	MOON Dec.	MOON d	MOON H.P.	Lat.	Twilight Naut.	Twilight Civil	Sunrise	Moonrise 20	Moonrise 21	Moonrise 22	Moonrise 23
20 00	179 38.8	N23 26.1	93 36.3	15.2	N 5 12.0	9.7	54.4	N 72	▓	▓	▓	11 25	13 01	14 37	16 17
01	194 38.6	26.1	108 10.5	15.2	5 02.3	9.7	54.4	N 70	▓	▓	▓	11 30	12 59	14 30	16 03
02	209 38.5	26.1	122 44.7	15.3	4 52.6	9.7	54.4	68	▓	▓	▓	11 33	12 58	14 24	15 51
03	224 38.4	26.1	137 19.0	15.3	4 42.9	9.8	54.4	66	▓	▓	▓	11 36	12 57	14 18	15 41
04	239 38.2	26.1	151 53.3	15.3	4 33.1	9.7	54.3	64	////	////	01 31	11 39	12 57	14 14	15 33
05	254 38.1	26.2	166 27.6	15.4	4 23.4	9.8	54.3	62	////	////	02 09	11 41	12 56	14 10	15 26
06	269 38.0	N23 26.2	181 02.0	15.3	N 4 13.6	9.8	54.3	60	////	00 49	02 36	11 44	12 55	14 07	15 20
07	284 37.8	26.2	195 36.3	15.4	4 03.8	9.8	54.3	N 58	////	01 40	02 56	11 45	12 55	14 04	15 15
08	299 37.7	26.2	210 10.7	15.4	3 54.0	9.8	54.3	56	////	02 10	03 13	11 47	12 54	14 02	15 10
F 09	314 37.6	26.2	224 45.1	15.4	3 44.2	9.8	54.3	54	00 45	02 33	03 27	11 48	12 54	13 59	15 06
R 10	329 37.4	26.2	239 19.5	15.5	3 34.4	9.8	54.3	52	01 32	02 51	03 40	11 50	12 53	13 57	15 02
I 11	344 37.3	26.3	253 54.0	15.4	3 24.6	9.9	54.3	50	02 00	03 06	03 51	11 51	12 53	13 56	14 59
D 12	359 37.1	N23 26.3	268 28.4	15.5	N 3 14.7	9.8	54.3	45	02 46	03 36	04 13	11 53	12 52	13 51	14 51
A 13	14 37.0	26.3	283 02.9	15.4	3 04.9	9.9	54.3	N 40	03 17	03 58	04 31	11 56	12 52	13 48	14 45
Y 14	29 36.9	26.3	297 37.3	15.5	2 55.0	9.9	54.3	35	03 40	04 17	04 46	11 57	12 51	13 45	14 40
15	44 36.7	26.3	312 11.8	15.5	2 45.1	9.8	54.3	30	03 58	04 32	04 59	11 59	12 51	13 43	14 35
16	59 36.6	26.3	326 46.3	15.5	2 35.3	9.9	54.3	20	04 28	04 57	05 21	12 02	12 50	13 38	14 27
17	74 36.5	26.3	341 20.8	15.5	2 25.4	9.9	54.3	N 10	04 50	05 17	05 40	12 04	12 49	13 34	14 20
18	89 36.3	N23 26.3	355 55.3	15.6	N 2 15.5	9.9	54.3	0	05 09	05 36	05 58	12 07	12 49	13 31	14 14
19	104 36.2	26.3	10 29.9	15.5	2 05.6	10.0	54.3	S 10	05 26	05 53	06 16	12 09	12 48	13 27	14 07
20	119 36.1	26.3	25 04.4	15.5	1 55.6	9.9	54.3	20	05 43	06 10	06 34	12 12	12 47	13 23	14 01
21	134 35.9	26.4	39 38.9	15.6	1 45.7	9.9	54.3	30	05 59	06 29	06 55	12 14	12 47	13 19	13 53
22	149 35.8	26.4	54 13.5	15.6	1 35.8	10.0	54.3	35	06 08	06 40	07 08	12 16	12 46	13 17	13 48
23	164 35.7	26.4	68 48.1	15.5	1 25.8	9.9	54.3	40	06 17	06 51	07 22	12 18	12 46	13 14	13 43
21 00	179 35.5	N23 26.4	83 22.6	15.6	N 1 15.9	9.9	54.3	45	06 28	07 05	07 39	12 20	12 45	13 11	13 38
01	194 35.4	26.4	97 57.2	15.6	1 06.0	10.0	54.3	S 50	06 39	07 21	08 00	12 23	12 45	13 07	13 31
02	209 35.2	26.4	112 31.8	15.5	0 56.0	9.9	54.3	52	06 45	07 29	08 10	12 24	12 44	13 05	13 28
03	224 35.1	26.4	127 06.3	15.6	0 46.1	10.0	54.3	54	06 50	07 37	08 21	12 25	12 44	13 03	13 24
04	239 35.0	26.4	141 40.9	15.6	0 36.1	10.0	54.3	56	06 57	07 46	08 33	12 26	12 44	13 01	13 20
								58	07 03	07 56	08 48	12 28	12 43	12 59	13 16

Suppose, for instance, that we need to know the GHA and Declination of the Moon at 20:28:19 UT on 20 June:-

GHA 20:00	25°04′.4 (v=+15′.5)
Increment for 28m19s	+ 6°45′.4
	31°49′.8
v correction	+ 7′.4
GHA 20:28:19	31°57′.2
Dec 20:00	N 1°55′.6 (d=-9.9)
d correction	− 4′.7
Dec 20:28:19	N 1°50′.9

(d is negative because the declination is reducing)

Astro Navigation Handbook   65

Correcting the Sextant Altitude of the Moon

Just like the Sun and Planets, the Sextant Altitude of the Moon may need to be corrected for six errors.

Index error and dip affect a Moon sight in much the same way as a Sun or planet sight:-

Index error: found by checking the Sextant

Dip: found from the Altitude Correction Tables in the Nautical Almanac

The other four are different:

Refraction: is included in the "Altitude Correction Tables - Moon" in the Nautical Almanac.

Semi-diameter: The moon is so close to the Earth that it appears to be about the same diameter as the Sun, so the fact that you are likely to be measuring the altitude of its upper or lower limb, rather than the middle of it, is quite significant. The situation is made more complicated by a phenomenon known as Augmentation.

Augmentation: Augmentation is caused by the fact that the Earth's radius is about 6400km. This means that an observer who sees the Moon directly overhead is 6400km closer to it than someone who sees it low on the horizon, so it appears slightly larger.

Parallax: an error of up to about one degree, also caused by the fact that the Moon is so close to the Earth that its position on the celestial sphere appears to vary slightly, depending where the observer happens to be.

In the Nautical Almanac, the corrections for refraction, semi-diameter, parallax are given in two parts, the first dealing with the components that are affected by the Apparent Altitude (refraction and augmentation and the second with those related to the HP (Parallax and Semi diameter).

CHAPTER 10

THE MOON

ALTITUDE CORRECTION TABLES 0°–35°—MOON

App. Alt.	0°–4° Corrⁿ	5°–9° Corrⁿ	10°–14° Corrⁿ	15°–19° Corrⁿ	20°–24° Corrⁿ	25°–29° Corrⁿ	30°–34° Corrⁿ	App. Alt.
00	0 33.8	5 58.2	10 62.1	15 62.8	20 62.2	25 60.8	30 58.9	00
10	35.9	58.5	62.2	62.8	62.1	60.8	58.8	10
20	37.8	58.7	62.2	62.8	62.1	60.7	58.8	20
30	39.6	58.9	62.3	62.8	62.1	60.7	58.7	30
40	41.2	59.1	62.3	62.8	62.0	60.6	58.6	40
50	42.6	59.3	62.4	62.7	62.0	60.6	58.5	50
00	1 44.0	6 59.5	11 62.4	16 62.7	21 62.0	26 60.5	31 58.5	00
10	45.2	59.7	62.4	62.7	61.9	60.4	58.4	10
20	46.3	59.9	62.5	62.7	61.9	60.4	58.3	20
30	47.3	60.0	62.5	62.7	61.9	60.3	58.2	30
40	48.3	60.2	62.5	62.7	61.8	60.3	58.2	40
50	49.2	60.3	62.6	62.7	61.8	60.2	58.1	50
00	2 50.0	7 60.5	12 62.6	17 62.7	22 61.7	27 60.1	32 58.0	00
10	50.8	60.6	62.6	62.6	61.7	60.1	57.9	10
20	51.4	60.7	62.6	62.6	61.6	60.0	57.8	20
30	52.1	60.9	62.7	62.6	61.6	59.9	57.8	30
40	52.7	61.0	62.7	62.6	61.5	59.9	57.7	40
50	53.3	61.1	62.7	62.6	61.5	59.8	57.6	50
00	3 53.8	8 61.2	13 62.7	18 62.5	23 61.5	28 59.7	33 57.5	00
10	54.3	61.3	62.7	62.5	61.4	59.7	57.4	10
20	54.8	61.4	62.7	62.5	61.4	59.6	57.4	20
30	55.2	61.5	62.8	62.5	61.3	59.6	57.3	30
40	55.6	61.6	62.8	62.4	61.3	59.5	57.2	40
50	56.0	61.6	62.8	62.4	61.2	59.4	57.1	50
00	4 56.4	9 61.7	14 62.8	19 62.4	24 61.2	29 59.3	34 57.0	00
10	56.7	61.8	62.8	62.3	61.1	59.3	56.9	10
20	57.1	61.9	62.8	62.3	61.1	59.2	56.9	20
30	57.4	61.9	62.8	62.3	61.0	59.1	56.8	30
40	57.7	62.0	62.8	62.2	60.9	59.1	56.7	40
50	57.9	62.1	62.8	62.2	60.9	59.0	56.6	50

H.P.	L U	L U	L U	L U	L U	L U	L U	H.P.
54.0	0.3 0.9	0.3 0.9	0.4 1.0	0.5 1.1	0.6 1.2	0.7 1.3	0.9 1.5	54.0
54.3	0.7 1.1	0.7 1.2	0.7 1.2	0.8 1.3	0.9 1.4	1.1 1.5	1.2 1.7	54.3
54.6	1.1 1.4	1.1 1.4	1.1 1.4	1.2 1.5	1.3 1.6	1.4 1.7	1.5 1.8	54.6
54.9	1.4 1.6	1.5 1.6	1.5 1.6	1.6 1.7	1.6 1.8	1.8 1.9	1.9 2.0	54.9
55.2	1.8 1.8	1.8 1.8	1.9 1.9	1.9 1.9	2.0 2.0	2.1 2.1	2.2 2.2	55.2
55.5	2.2 2.0	2.2 2.0	2.3 2.1	2.3 2.1	2.4 2.2	2.4 2.3	2.5 2.4	55.5
55.8	2.6 2.2	2.6 2.2	2.6 2.3	2.7 2.3	2.7 2.4	2.8 2.4	2.9 2.5	55.8
56.1	3.0 2.4	3.0 2.5	3.0 2.5	3.0 2.5	3.1 2.6	3.1 2.6	3.2 2.7	56.1
56.4	3.4 2.7	3.4 2.7	3.4 2.7	3.4 2.7	3.4 2.8	3.5 2.8	3.5 2.9	56.4

Astro Navigation Handbook

CHAPTER 10

In the second part of the table, the corrections for the Upper and Lower Limb are different, so they are given separately. In what might be regarded as a rather awkward attempt to "simplify" matters, the compilers of the almanac have kept all the corrections positive by adding an arbitrary 30 minutes to the figures given for the upper limb.

This means that we now have to remember to subtract the extra 30 minutes from the altitude of the Upper Limb!

Suppose, for instance, that the Sextant altitude of the Moon's Upper Limb was 32°47′.9. The sextant was 3.2 m above the waterline, and had an index error of 5′.3 on the arc, and the HP given in the Nautical Almanac was 54′.3.

Start by correcting the Sextant Altitude for Index error and dip as usual:

Sextant Altitude	32°47′.9
Index error	− 5′.3
Observed Altitude	32°42′.6
Dip	− 3′.1
Apparent Altitude	32°39′.5

Then in the top half of the Altitude Correction table, use the degrees of the Apparent Altitude to find the relevant column and the minutes of Apparent Altitude to find the right row, to pick out the first of the two corrections.

Stay in the same column, but use the HP to locate the correct row in the lower part of the table, to find the second correction. The column is divided with headings "L" (for Lower") and "U" (for "Upper"): in this particular case, where the sight was of the upper limb, we obviously need the "Upper" value.

Apparent Altitude	32°39′.5
First correction	+ 57′.7
Second correction	+ 1′.7
	33°38′.9

And finally, because this particular example concerns a sight of the moon's upper limb, we need to apply the special upper limb correction by subtracting 30 minutes.

	33°38′.9
Upper limb correction	− 30′.0
True Altitude	33°08′.9

Appendix 1: Plotting Sheets

Astro plotting sheets, with a rudimentary graticule of meridians and parallels but no coastlines, landmarks, or contours – are available from various official and commercial sources.

But they are not the only option. There is no reason why you shouldn't plot an astro fix on any ordinary navigational chart of a suitable scale, so long as it covers the right latitude: you can always re-label the meridians of longitude, and ignore the hydrographic information.

Another possibility is to draw your own plotting sheet:

1. On a suitable sheet of paper, draw a vertical line. This will become a meridian, and can usefully be marked off with a scale of latitude at any convenient scale (three millimetres per minute of latitude is suitable on A4 paper).

2. Draw horizontal lines from the top and bottom of the latitude scale. These will become parallels of latitude.

3. Draw a sloping line from where the meridian drawn in step 1 intersects with one of the parallels. The angle between the sloping line and the parallel corresponds to the latitude to which you want the plotting sheet to apply. e.g. in the example, the centre of the plotting sheet is at 50°30, so the line slopes upwards at 50°30.

4. Measure along the sloping line, and mark a distance of 60 miles from the intersection between the meridian and the parallel. e.g. if the scale chosen in step 1 was 3mm per minute, the sloping line should be marked at 3 x 60=180mm.

5. Through the mark made in step 4, draw another vertical line. This represents the next meridian.

6. Divide one of the parallels into sixths and sixtieths, to form a scale of longitude. It is unlikely that the distance between meridians will be a convenient multiple of 60, so the simplest way to achieve this may be to mark the sloping line from step 3 with an exact copy of the latitude scale, and to drop verticals from each mark to meet the parallel of latitude.

7. Label the meridians and parallels.

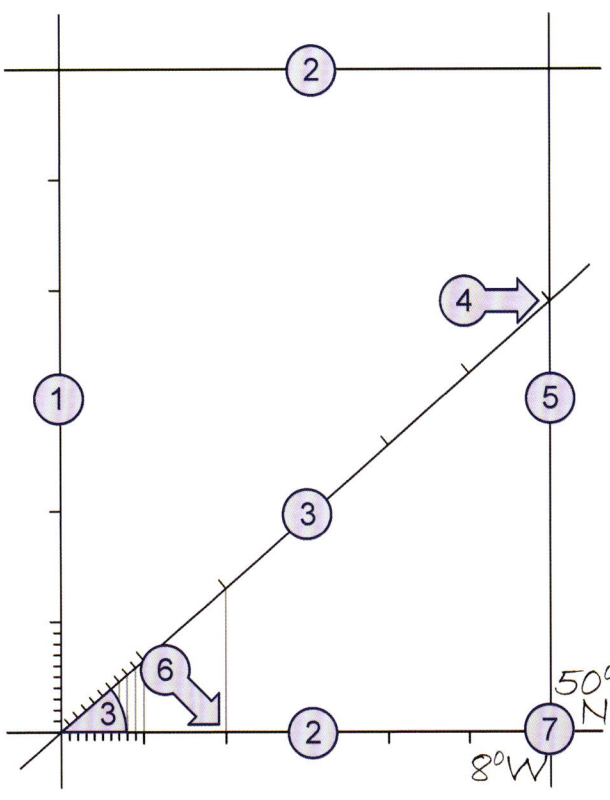

GLOSSARY

Altitude		The angle between an observer's line of sight to a heavenly body and the horizon.
Altitude	**Apparent**	The sextant altitude, corrected for index error and dip.
Altitude	**Calculated**	The altitude of a heavenly body, obtained by calculation.
Altitude	**Observed**	The sextant altitude, corrected for index error.
Altitude	**Sextant**	The altitude measured by a sextant.
Altitude	**True**	The measured altitude of a heavenly body, after all corrections have been applied.
Augmentation		A special correction applied only to sights of the Moon. See page 66.
Azimuth		The true bearing of a heavenly body, as seen by an observer at or near the surface of the Earth.
Chosen Position		An arbitrary position close to the vessel's EP, chosen to make the calculation of an astro fix as simple as was possible.
Declination		The angle between the celestial equator and a heavenly body, comparable with Latitude on the Earth's surface.
Dip		An error in the measurement of altitude, caused by the fact that an observer's line of sight to the horizon is always slightly below horizontal.
Ecliptic		The path apparently traced out by the Sun during the course of a year as it travels round the Celestial Sphere.
Estimated Position		A vessel's position based upon the direction and distance it has moved from its last known position, allowing for the effects of leeway, tidal streams and ocean currents.
First Point of Aries		The point at which the Sun crosses the Celestial Equator at the onset of the Northern summer, used as a reference for the position of stars.
Greenwich Hour Angle	**GHA**	The angle between the Prime (Greenwich) Meridian and the meridian on which a heavenly body lies, comparable with Longitude on the Earth's surface.
Greenwich Mean Time	**GMT**	The old name for Universal time.
H_c		Common abbreviation for Calculated Altitude.
H_o		Common abbreviation for True Altitude.
HP		See Parallax - Horizontal.
Index error		The error of a sextant caused by misalignment of the index mirror.
Intercept		The distance between the Chosen Position and the Position Circle.
Local Hour Angle		The angle between the observer's meridian (or their Chosen Position) and the meridian on which a heavenly body lies.
Marcq St Hilaire		A nineteenth century French Captain, credited with devising what is now the most common method for plotting an astro navigation sight.
Meridian Passage		The moment at which a heavenly body crosses the observer's meridian.
Nautical Almanac		A reference book that gives astronomical data such as the position of the Sun, planets, stars, and moon, and the times of sunrise, sunset, and twilight.

GLOSSARY

Parallax — A correction applied to the apparent altitude of a heavenly body, to account for the fact that it is being observed from the surface of the Earth, rather than from the centre of the celestial sphere.

Parallax   Horizontal — The value of parallax for a body which appears to be on the horizon, given in the Nautical Almanac as a basis from which to calculate the actual parallax.

Perpendicularity — A sextant check, to ensure that the index mirror is perpendicular to the frame.

PZX triangle — A triangle on the surface of the celestial sphere, whose vertices are the celestial pole, the zenith at the chosen position, and the heavenly body.

Refraction — An error in the measurement of altitude, caused by light from a heavenly body being bent (refracted) as it passes through the Earth's atmosphere.

Semi diameter — Half the apparent angular diameter of a body such as the Sun or Moon, applied as a correction to account for the fact that a sextant altitude invariably measures the altitude of either the lower or upper edge of the body, rather than its centre.

Seven Selected Stars — The subtitle and common name for the Air Sight Reduction Tables Volume 1.

Side error — An error of a sextant caused by misalignment of the horizon glass.

Siderial Hour Angle — The angle between the First Point of Aries and the meridian on which a heavenly body lies.

Sight Reduction Tables — Tables containing the answers to pre-computed astro-nav calculations.

Sight Reduction Tables   Air — Sight reduction tables intended for aviation use, typically offering a precision of 1′. Now popular for yacht and small ship navigation.

Sight Reduction Tables   Marine — Sight reduction tables intended for marine use, typically offering a precision of 0′.1.

Twilight — A period during which the Sun is below the horizon but the sky is not completely dark.

Twilight   Astronomical — The time at which the sun is eighteen degrees below the horizon.

Twilight   Civil — The time at which the sun is six degrees below the horizon.

Twilight   Nautical — The time at which the sun is twelve degrees below the horizon.

Universal Time   UT — The politically correct term for what used to be known as Greenwich Mean Time.

Universal Time Coordinated   UTC — Coordinated Universal Time: time measured by very accurate clocks, periodically realigned with UT

Zenith — The point on the celestial sphere that is directly overhead, as seen by an observer on Earth.

Zenith Distance — The angular distance between a heavenly body and the observer's zenith.

Zenith Distance   Calculated — The angular distance between a heavenly body and the zenith of a chosen position, obtained by calculation.

Zenith Distance   True — The angular distance between a heavenly body and the observer's zenith, obtained by subtracting the true altitude of the body from ninety degrees.

INDEX

Alkaid	58
Alpheratz	58
Altair	58-59
altitude, apparent	50, 59, 63, 66, 68
Altitude, Calculated ("tabulated") (H_c)	35, 38, 39, 41, 51, 54, 55, 57, 59
mnemonic for	39
altitude, sextant	43, 46-47, 50, 54, 59, 63, 66-68
Altitude, True (H_o)	38, 39, 50, 51, 54, 55, 59, 63
altitude angle	7
Arcturus	52, 53, 54, 56, 58-59
Aries, First Point of	53-54
Aries, Local Hour Angle of	57, 58, 59, 63
augmentation	66
Azimuth	35, 38-40, 41, 57
Bermuda	20
Betelgeuse	56
Campbell, John	19
celestial equator	14
celestial poles, North and South	14
celestial sphere	14-18, 52
finding Declination of the Sun	17-18
finding Greenwich Hour Angle and Declination of other bodies	18
finding Greenwich Hour Angle of the Sun	15-16
chronometer, invention of	19
compass, check by	42
Coordinated Universal Time (UTC)	20
Copernicus, Nicolaus	14
Daylight Saving Time	22
Declination (Dec)	14, 15, 17-18, 29, 32, 44-45, 50, 53, 54, 65
Dip (error)	30-31, 36, 46-47, 50, 54, 59, 63, 66, 68
Earth, orbit and rotation of	19-20, 53
Earth, shape of	33
First Point of Aries	53-54
fix, running	40-41
Galileo Galilei	14
Greenwich Hour Angle (GHA)	14, 15-16, 18, 34, 43, 44-45, 50, 51, 53, 54, 65
Greenwich Mean Time (GMT)	20
Greenwich Meridian and observatory	20, 21, 25
Hadley, John	19
Hamilton, Bermuda	20
Harrison, John	19
Index error	12-13, 30-31, 36, 46, 50, 54, 59, 63, 66, 68
"on/off the arc"	13, 31
residual	12
intercept	33, 38-40, 51, 54, 59
International Earth Rotation and Reference Systems Service	20
International Standards Organisation	22
Jupiter	43, 49, 50
Kochab	58
latitude, calculating from noon sight	29, 32
Local Hour Angle (LHA)	34-35, 36, 51, 54
of Aries	57, 58, 59, 63
formulae	35
Mars	43, 46, 49

INDEX

Meridian, Greenwich	20, 21, 25
Meridian Passage (Mer.Pass.)	20, 24, 48-49
Mirfak	58, 59
Moon sights	43, 64-68
advantage/disadvantages of	64
correcting sextant altitude of	66-68
finding Greenwich Hour Angle and Declination	65
Nautical Almanac, The	
Altitude Correction Tables	46, 66, 67-68
Daily Page	15, 17
error corrections	30-31, 36
finding Declination of the Sun	17-18
finding solar noon	24-25
finding sunrise, sunset and twilight	26-27
and Greenwich Hour Angle	15, 16
Increments and Corrections tables	16, 17, 18, 45, 50, 53-54
and the moon	65, 66, 67-68
and planets	44-45, 46, 48, 49, 50
Polaris Tables	61-63
and stars	52, 53-54
noon, when is it?	19, 24-25
noon sight	28-32
arithmetic	30-32
geometry	29
octant, invention of	19
parallax (error)	30, 31, 46-47, 66
planet sights	43-51
calculation	50-51
correcting Sextant Altitude	43, 46-47
finding Greenwich Hour Angle and Declination	44-45
planning	48-49
planispheres	56-57
Polaris	61-63
principles, basic	5-6
PZX triangle	34
Rasalhague	58, 59
Reeds Astro Navigation Tables see also Nautical Almanac, The	22
refraction (error)	30, 31, 46-47, 50, 54, 59, 63, 66
Rigel	56
running fix	40-41
St Hilaire, Marcq	33-34
Saturn	43, 49
semi-diameter (error)	30, 31, 36, 46-47, 66
sextant, adjusting	10-13 see also index error
perpendicularity	10
side error	11
sextant, check for vertical	8
sextant, development of	19
sextant, operation of	7
sextant, parts of	7
clamp	7, 8, 9, 10
horizon glass	7, 11, 12
index arm	7, 8, 9, 10, 11, 12
index mirror	7, 9, 10, 12
micrometer	7, 8, 9, 11, 12, 13, 28
scale	7, 9, 10, 12, 13
shades	7, 8
telescope	7, 8, 9, 10, 11
sextant, reading	9
sextant, satisfaction in handling	5
sextant, shooting stars or planets	9
sextant, shooting the Sun	8
sextant, tips for using	13
sextant, types of	7
Sextant Altitude	28, 30, 36, 43, 46-47
Sidereal Hour Angle	53, 54

INDEX

sight reduction by calculator	41-42
Sight Reduction Tables	34, 41, 49, 54
Air	34, 35-38, 55
"Correction to Tabulated Altitude for Minutes of Declination"	37-38
using	37-38
Volume 1 see stars, "Seven Selected"	
Marine	34, 55
star sights see also Polaris	
precomputed	56
preparing for	55
principle of	52-55
"simultaneous"	60
starfinders	56-57
stars	
morning and evening	52-60
identifying	56-57
"Seven Selected"	52, 57-60
star sights, preparing for	55
star sights, principle of	52-55
navigating by	5-6
"Seven Selected"	52, 57-60
Summer Time	22
Sun	
compass check by	42
Ecliptic (path)	53
finding Declination	17-18, 32
finding Greenwich Hour Angle	15-16
Sun sight, noon see noon sight	
Sun sights, morning and afternoon	33-42
Azimuth	35, 38-40, 41
compass check	42
intercept	33, 38-40
Local Hour Angle (LHA)	34-35, 36
PZX triangle	34
running fix	40-41
St Hilaire method	33-34
sight reduction by calculator	41-42
Sight Reduction Tables see Sight Reduction Tables	
sunrise and sunset	26
time	19-27
Coordinated Univeral (UTC)	20
"Equation of"	20, 24 see also Meridian Passage
noon	19, 24-25
solar	19-20
Summer	22
sunrise and sunset	26
twilight, civil and nautical	26-27, 55, 58
Universal (UT)	20
time of transit	20 see also Meridian Passage
time zones	20-22
maritime	21
naming	22
twilight, civil and nautical	26-27, 55, 58
Universal Time (UT) and Universal Time, Coordinated (UTC)	20
Venus	43, 44, 46, 47, 49
Weems and Plath Starfinder 2102-D	57
zenith	5-6, 14
Zenith Distance	29, 31, 33

NOTES

NOTES

NOTES

NOTES

NOTES